T0065430

A JOURNEY INTO THE UNKNOWN

EXPERIENCES WITH DIVINE INTERVENTION

V R

BALBOA.PRESS

A DIVISION OF HAY HOUSE

Balboa Press books may be ordered through booksellers or by contacting:

Balboa Press
A Division of Hay House
1663 Liberty Drive
Bloomington, IN 47403
www.balboapress.com
844-682-1282

Because of the dynamic nature of the Internet, any web addresses or
links contained in this book may have changed since publication and
may no longer be valid. The views expressed in this work are solely those
of the author and do not necessarily reflect the views of the publisher,
and the publisher hereby disclaims any responsibility for them.

The author of this book does not dispense medical advice or prescribe the use
of any technique as a form of treatment for physical, emotional, or medical
problems without the advice of a physician, either directly or indirectly. The
intent of the author is only to offer information of a general nature to help
you in your quest for emotional and spiritual well-being. In the event you use
any of the information in this book for yourself, which is your constitutional
right, the author and the publisher assume no responsibility for your actions.

Any people depicted in stock imagery provided by Getty Images are
models, and such images are being used for illustrative purposes only.
Certain stock imagery © Getty Images.

Interior Image Credit: VR

Print information available on the last page.

ISBN: 978-1-9822-6419-2 (sc)
ISBN: 978-1-9822-6420-8 (e)

Balboa Press rev. date: 02/26/2021

Dedication

This book is dedicated to all the light bulbs in my life.

INTRODUCTION

MY BELOVED GURU FOUND ME and paved the way towards self- realization. Then he gave me his blessings to write about my experiences on this journey with him. If I were to describe myself, I would say, I am uncomplicated, quiet and hard working. I was never a religious person but I studied the Bible in high school and believed that God is watching over me. I led a normal life until my Guru intervened and everything took a turn for the better. I am an ordinary person who got lucky when my Guru gave me the extraordinary opportunity to transform my life. I believe, with the illuminating grace of a perfect spiritual master this can happen to anyone.

This miraculous journey took years and it happened in various stages. In each one of them, I received guidance in the form of words, which captivated me. Words travelled unexpectedly into my thoughts, sometimes as questions, sentences or phrases. They circulated constantly, which to me was an extraordinary method of forcing me to pay attention. At the end of each stage, he gave me the guidance that I needed to grow and evolve in every way.

I grew up as a farmer's daughter in Guyana, South America with five sisters and one brother. Our life was simple, good, and required a lot of hard work but we were content. There was always an abundance of fresh fruits and vegetables in our home. My father was a tall, strong man who enjoyed fishing and supplied my mother with fresh fish, which she often fried or dried because we didn't have a refrigerator back then. Whenever we helped our parents in our rice fields and the farm, they would allow us to fish during our lunch breaks and sometimes, we caught enough fish for the next day's meal. I can still taste those lunches as if it was yesterday. Fried eggplant with potatoes, tomatoes and fried fish with rice, or stewed dried fish and fried, leafy green mustard with shrimp and rice. Lunch tasted so good, after working for hours in the blazing hot sun.

Our farm was in a different location far from home. We travelled on road with our donkey cart for about one hour and then with a canoe on water for another hour. It was fun travelling in the canoe but we had to sit still to prevent the canoe from overturning. We were fascinated by the schools of tiny silver fishes, darting here and there in the clear, calm, sand colored water. At the farm, my sisters and I would help our parents with planting and when it was time to reap the fruits and vegetables, we were their helpers. We never refused our parents, and felt it was our duty to help them any which way we could. The main crops at the farm were pumpkin, corn, black eye peas, hot peppers, bananas, plantains sweet potatoes and eddoes. Occasionally, my father would find ripe papayas or a bunch of ripe short bananas, while we were at the farm and these would be our treats for the day. I always enjoyed eating, a freshly picked ripe papaya or a ripe banana from the tree. To me, they tasted better and sweeter. This was how we lived then, children worked together with their parents and helped them. Now as adults, most of us have green thumbs and still enjoy fishing and planting.

My mother, was half my father's size but she worked just as hard and took care of their seven children. She was talented in so many areas. She sewed all our clothes and she was an amazing cook. We were always excited when the holidays arrived. I can still remember the mouthwatering homemade fruit and black cakes, ginger beer, banana fritters, bara (lentil fritter) eaten with a chutney dip, boiled and fried chick peas and goja (spiced coconut turnover). I learned to cook, bake and sew by watching her and copied her way of doing things.

She was also the driving force behind our education because she wanted us to have a better life. My job every morning at sunrise, was to make the beds and sweep the house before I leave for high school. If I had a test the following day, I would study the whole night until five 0'clock in the morning, and while sweeping, held the broom with one hand and my book with the other. Brooms in those days were made from coconut branches. I really had to study, to do well in school. I was never the smartest in class, I usually came in third or fourth and that was good enough for me and my parents. Every evening, I would iron my school uniform with a flat iron, and every pleat on my skirt had to be in its precise place. My mother liked our surroundings to be clean and neat and all of us are like her. She was so very happy when my sister and I became teachers.

When I started teaching, my mother became very sick and died, leaving my father with three teenage daughters to care for. My aunts decided to marry me off since I was the eldest one at home. They didn't force me and soon after, I was married to the son of my aunt's best friend. My mother-in-law was a well-known tailor who sewed and dressed hundreds of brides. Without any measurements, she sewed a couple of my dresses and they were a perfect fit. She was one of a kind. She attended church regularly with my aunt and was a very loving and kind person. She was also very generous with others and often offered food and a place to stay. We all admired and loved her dearly. For me she is irreplaceable. After marriage, I taught until my first child was born and then became a stay at home mom. My husband held a management position and we lived a comfortable life for a few years. Then the country struggled to attain economic independence, which led to a crises and many people began leaving the country in order to survive. I was one of them.

During the younger years of my life, there was no indication that a Guru would rescue and take me on an unknown journey to attain the ultimate knowledge. I was always introverted, a quiet, easy going and obedient child. I did my chores and took my studies seriously. This enormous transition that was written and sealed, before I was born by our Master Crafter God, was an unexpected giant explosion of rainbow colors within me. I became settled and more spiritual than I ever expected to be.

I arrived in the United States of America in 1976, and lived with my sister and brother-in-law in Corona, Queens. It was heart wrenching to leave my family in Guyana. I was always worried about them. The hope for a better life made me strong and deep down, I knew that this was the sacrifice we had to make as a family. I was ready to find a job quickly and fortunately, with the help of my sister, I found a job as a nanny and the family sponsored me. Two years later, I received my green card and my family was able to join me in this great country. Soon after, my nanny job was terminated because the family moved to Colorado. Then, I found a job assembling jewelry displays in a factory and worked there for five years.

During my last year at this factory, I started to experience some changes in my life. I felt ill every day and couldn't go to work, so I had to leave this job. Sometimes it was a migraine headache and other times, I felt weak and just stayed in bed. I couldn't cook a meal or even wash a teacup. I used over the counter medication and hoped that after a while it would go away. My husband never complained and tried to help me as much as possible. Although I didn't know it at the time, this was the onset of my encounter with divine intervention, and my eventual transformation. What followed was an unexpected journey to discover my potential. I was guided towards educating myself further, to build confidence and self-reliance. More importantly, through meditation, I received the spiritual guidance necessary to walk on the path of knowing myself. Growing up, I never imagined that God's plan for me meant immigrating to America to not only build a new life but a new me.

For me, my journey began with words, words that travelled from God and landed in my mind as clues on a map leading to a hidden treasure. Words that were simple but became a magnetic force in my life, pulling me towards God and unravelling his plan. Words that I consider my well-wishers and good fortune. Words that taught me how to admire and respect everyone's achievements. Words that gave me hope, when I was confused and wondered what would happen next. Words that lifted me up, when I thought that my life was going downhill. Words that followed me everywhere and taught me to be a better person. Words that became my trusted friends. Words that gave me wisdom and the strength to reach for the stars. Words that remind me every day not to forget those who helped me. Words made me realize that because of God, I was surrounded by good people. For me, these words were droppings from heaven and now, I am emotionally attached to them. I feel like they are a part of me.

My Tribute to Words

Old words, new words, words, words and more words racing through my mind. The result, a unique experience manifested itself and a path to self - realization was revealed.

Accessible	Adapt	Affection	Ambience	Audience	Awesome	Behest
	Behaviors	Bewilder	Caliber	Compassion	Concern	
Compelled	Counselor	Crown	Dedicated	Deserve	Descending	Destiny
	Diamond	Dismayed	Energy	Etchings	Experiences	
Enjoy	Freedom	Feathers	Forget	Forgive	Geared	Goals
	Happiness	Hesitated	Hovered	Innocently	Inspiration	Guidance
Inspire	Intervention	Journey	Knowledge	Ladder	Lining	Meditation
	Memorizing	Messages	Mindset	Miracles	Musicians	
Noble	Obligated	Observing	Opportunity	Open	Patience	Pondered
	Positive	Positioned	Professional	Possibilities	Quality	
Rare	Recognition	Reeling	Rekindle	Represent	Scrutiny	Showered
	Spirituality	Tenderness	Tranquility	Tolerance	Tumble	
Thunder	Purity	Umbrellas	Well-Wishers	Willingly	Wind	Wisdom

CHAPTER ONE

The Voice From Within

I HAD MY FIRST SPIRITUAL experience in 1984. I was thirty-two years old with two young children and a husband. At the time, I didn't realize it was the beginning of my walk towards the kingdom of God. When I was younger, I thought only nuns and missionary workers were the special kind of people who received gifts from above but I was wrong.

I remember clearly, that I was alone at home on my birthday and it was snowing. My two daughters were at school and my husband went to work. I stood by my living room window silently admiring the snowflakes and for the very first time, I heard a voice from within saying something different from what I was used to hearing. It said, *within me is a heart filled with gold, a mind as pure as the falling snow and the mind determines the quality of a person*. To me they were not only poetic words but represented illuminating lights peeking out of an invisible pathway. I knew they came

1

from God and I was stunned into stillness as the words kept repeating themselves.

After a couple of days, I felt a possessiveness for these words, as if they were my treasures to guard. Afraid of forgetting them, I wrote them in a note book for safekeeping. Surprisingly, once they were written, I stopped hearing them. For years, I pondered the meaning of this statement and wondered what this was all about. After years of meditating and praying, this time, when the question arose, the answer followed like an obedient child. I was surprised at this effortless revelation which occurred, when I was busy cleaning. This was a birthday gift from God, a divine message revealing his plan to take me on a journey of transformation. Then when my Guru came, he gave me the technique to realize my true nature, purity of heart and mind. I was so humbled by his selfless commitment to humanity. In my Guru's shelter, I felt like I had been grabbed from the streets and placed in a palace to rule over a kingdom with no prior knowledge or experience. I thought only the embodiment of love itself could have such mercy on all beings.

One morning, a few months later, I had another unexpected experience. I heard loud footsteps, slowly stomping on the parquet floors in my living room, as I was leaving my apartment for work. I looked around and didn't see anything or anyone, yet somehow I wasn't afraid. Then when I arrived at work that day, I heard the same loud footsteps as I entered the building. I thought this was strange but focused on my work instead and the footsteps were soon forgotten. These foot-steps were my first indication that an invisible body guard had arrived, to guide me towards advancement. A couple of weeks later, I felt an unquenchable drive to read and educate myself and to think beyond factory work.

Working in the factory was tedious and I wanted to find a better job. I thought of taking professional courses but I couldn't afford to spend money on educating myself. I knew we could never survive on one salary but my mind was constantly nagging me to do something to better myself. One afternoon after work, I decided to go to the library. I borrowed books about topics that I liked. Books about art and crafts, painting, gardening, and cook books. I began experimenting with different sewing materials, cooking approaches and gained new skills. This was also the beginning of some mysterious happenings at home. Every week, something broke or simply stopped working. Our electric kettle, our iron, our toaster, our vacuum, and our floor lamp, all broke, one after the other. This pattern continued for months, making me worried and frustrated. We were struggling to make ends meet and couldn't afford to replace the items. As things continued to break, I felt that our life was moving backward instead of going forward.

Around this time, I started suffering from migraines. My head would hurt for two days and on the third day the pain would disappear, leaving my body feeling exhausted. Eventually, because of this, I couldn't go to work and had to leave my job. There were days when I couldn't get out of bed or do any chores at home. My children would help me, and whenever they saw me looking worried, they would dance to make me laugh. When I didn't have the headaches, I had a bad cold, and the coughing lingered for weeks and sounded awful. I often asked myself during this period, *when will I be healthy again*? I was tired of being sick. I was young and eager to work. I wanted to help my husband provide a decent life for our children, but I couldn't. I found it difficult to eat and other times, I felt tremendous anxiety. My friends were willing to help me, but I didn't know what was wrong. I couldn't explain my sickness, and they were worried. I looked unhealthy, pale, and gaunt. I went to the doctor several times and returned with a prescription but the treatment never worked.

Sometimes I couldn't sleep at night, and I would lay in bed staring at the walls. Then on one of those sleepless nights, I had the urge to write and later writing became an obsession. I wrote about everything that was bothering me at the time, and it seemed, like I was pouring my heart out. This gave me a sense of relief, and diverted my attention away from my health issues. There was a lot of complaining in my writings, but among them were also words of wisdom, which gave me hope that something good would eventually surface in my life. I've learned that whenever unwelcome thoughts creep in, I should find a way to shift my attention to other activities.

One night, I was laying on my bed and couldn't sleep. After tossing and turning for a while, I got up, and I wrote, *when two minds are connected, a resourceful mind will emerge.* Now I understand the meaning of these words. They were telling me that connecting to the limitless knowledge of my Guru, would produce resourcefulness in me and that is exactly what happened. He awakened my ability to think creatively, so that I could adapt and find solutions in all situations. Throughout this journey, this has been the recurring theme. Every time, I thought I couldn't resolve a problem, he would step in and show me in my visions an alternative resolution.

Even though I didn't have the ability to hold a job, I felt an overwhelming boredom and restlessness to be at home. Somehow, I still had the desire to push myself to do something. I didn't want to waste any time, so I decided to take free typing classes at the local high school. The class met three times a week, and the course lasted three months. On the first day, while I was walking to class, a surprise appeared when I was one block away from the school. I saw a young woman, dressed beautifully in a red and gold saree and recognized her as a Hindu goddess. Unlike the footsteps, this time, I saw a clear image of a beautiful Goddess. She was walking in front of me and I felt as if she was accompanying me to class. Once I entered the building, she disappeared and I didn't see her again.

During class that day, my hands seemed to be powered by an electrical energy. My fingers were tapping the keys like a runner sprinting towards the finish line. It was so fast that I couldn't keep up with the correct spelling of the words. I was astonished, and so were others. That night, I remembered the sight of the saintly being and I was still in shock at the speed of my fingers moving on the keys. I took this as a sign that God would give me the energy to master new skills and this gave me the motivation to continue. My mother always said, that no one can steal education and I felt like God was encouraging me. The following day, a teacher was assigned to sit behind me to observe my typing speed but it was back to normal.

When I completed the course, the idea of joining the workforce weighed heavily on my mind all the time.

Although I was ready mentally, I was still very weak physically. Knowing that I couldn't work, bothered me but I listened to my body's signals and stayed home for a while longer, nursing myself back to being healthy and strong. In Guyana my parents owned a farm and rice fields. Growing up in this environment meant, we always had something to do and no time for idling. I am thankful to my parents for instilling a strong work ethic in their children. They taught us through their own example, that hard work always produced good results and I didn't want to disappoint their values.

CHAPTER TWO

Learning Something New

ONE AFTERNOON, I WAS READING the newspaper and saw an ad from an art, and advertising design school. At the time, I still didn't understand what was happening to me and I felt uneasy to be alone at home. Despite not knowing anything about this field, I saw it as an escape route to be with other people and simultaneously educate myself. The other students were much younger than I was, but it didn't bother me. After using a large part of our savings for the tuition, I was determined to gain knowledge, and paid close attention to everything I was taught in class. Three months into the course, I was practicing font designs and basic drawing. When I couldn't sleep at night, I would write or draw. I didn't know then that the writings and drawings would be a part of a story.

During this course, I had to learn to draw the human body by looking at nude models. I didn't know at that time, that it was included in the program. Then one day, a female model was posing naked in the class room. I think the lack of exposure in my strict and sheltered upbringing, made me feel out of my comfort zone. I was uncomfortable with the nudity. Half way into the course and after a lot of thinking, I knew that the best thing for me to do, was to quit. I was disappointed. I consoled myself by being grateful that I had learned so much, in such a short time. The creative ideas that were planted had taken root and continued to thrive. The letters of the alphabet lingered in my thoughts and wouldn't go away. They were like magnets, pulling at my heart strings as if saying, *resume with your drawings.*

This feeling from within, spurred me onward to create numerous designs and it became one of my passions. The first letter I designed was a magnificent letter A. When I looked at it, I saw steps going upward and experienced a feeling of accomplishment. The finished design of this letter, brought a glimmer of light in my life and instead of sitting around doing nothing, I had something to do. I ran with the new ideas as they entered my mind. It affirmed, that my time wasn't wasted and reminded me of my mother's words, that knowledge gained can always be utilized.

Cry Water Eve and Comp

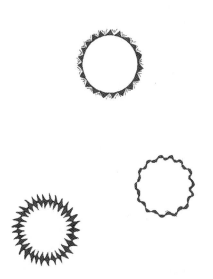

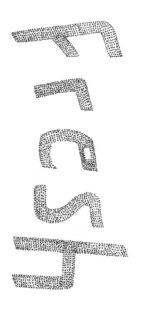

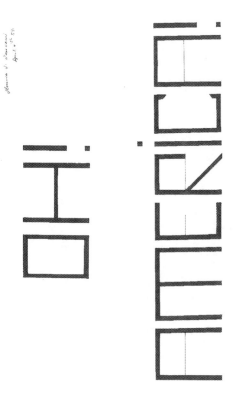

OH! AMERICA!

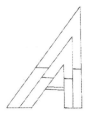

Florence V. Ransom.
May 15th 84

Audrye
Young
Roman
THE IN
Tall Bill

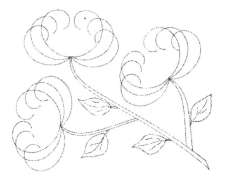

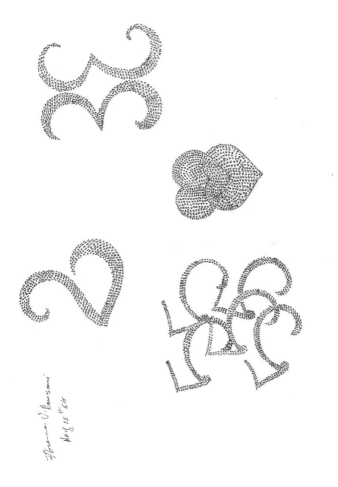

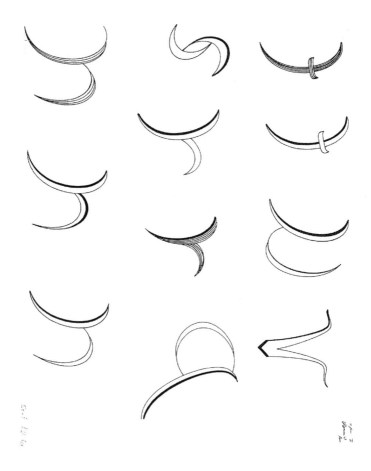

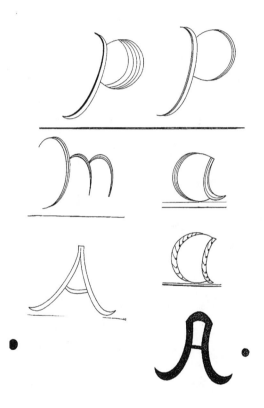

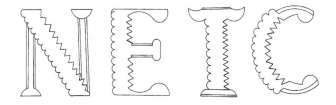

F. V. Ransome. April, 1894.

F V. Ransome April' 21st 94.

V. Ransome March 22nd 94.

28

trees

April 1984

These designs were completed in quick succession. I was shocked by my competence. I knew someone was helping me, but who and why? Looking at them now, I understand that with effort and a little help from the divine, one's potential is infinite. I never thought of myself as artistic but God knew better and opened the door to an opportunity, for me to discover something new about myself.

The one thing that still haunted me was how to regain my vitality, and peace of mind. I was always worried about my situation and felt helpless, not knowing how to come out of it. My main concern was for my children and the thought of not being able to do anything for them was excruciating. For more than a year, I felt I was in limbo between discovering new skills and the uncertainty of my health.

Then one day, we visited a family friend who offered me some advice which proved to be beneficial. She suggested that I should change my lifestyle and become more spiritual. She said praying and making sacrifices will help me to overcome any obstacle. I was willing to try anything because I desperately wanted to feel like myself again. From then on, I began my day with prayers. My mission was to eliminate all my depressive and negative thoughts and replaced them with thoughts of God. I was praying all the time and promised God that I would change my way of life and become more devoted. My daughters were ten and eight years old. I didn't want to leave them without a mother.

CHAPTER THREE

The Turning Point

MY PRAYERS WERE ANSWERED A short time later, when I received an unforeseen message. I was asleep on my sofa one day and had a dream. In my dream, there was a high mound of soil, and suddenly an older woman rushed into the soil and a second later, a younger woman walked out leisurely. This dream marked a turning point in my life because soon after, my health gradually improved. My body was feeling stronger and I felt guided to maintain a vegetarian diet, which helped me to feel more balanced.

A few weeks later, I had an unforgettable vision while resting at home one afternoon. I saw myself floating up into the clouds and everything surrounding me was white. I stopped ascending, and a man accompanied by a woman dressed in white appeared in front of me. I stood still, in numbed silence staring at them. I saw his features clearly but hers were hidden. The man reached forward and placed a gold crown on my head and then they both disappeared.

In that moment, I thought he must be God because who else would think that I am worthy. I didn't realize how magnanimous this act of God was. He was showing me in this vision, that he would lead me to self – knowledge. After having this vision, I had the feeling that my life would become better and that God would always be there to guide me.

After two months, I went to an employment agency and found a job in a jewelry factory. There I met a few people from my country and during our lunch breaks, we would exchange stories and jokes with one another. Even though, I enjoyed working at the factory and meeting some people from my country, there was a secret yearning for a better job. I knew that God would help me to find a better job and also help me to stay healthy. I continued to pray and followed a strict vegetarian diet during working hours. Whenever I thought my life was spiraling downward, divine intervention diverted these challenges to shift my inner compass towards God. Having God in my life was like a celebration every day and I was overwhelmed with gratitude by his continued generosity.

Christmas holidays were a joyous occasion, which I looked forward to when I was growing up. We didn't receive toys but my mother baked mouthwatering cakes and prepared special dishes for the holidays. This continued until I was older and could afford to exchange gifts with family and friends. When I had my own children, I continued with the tradition of baking and preparing special dishes. I enjoyed wrapping the gifts and placing them under the Christmas tree and during this time, we thoroughly cleaned and decorated our house for the holidays. I always admired our live tree and the festive decorations infusing our home with the joy of Christmas. Over the years, this feeling increased because I would receive a special gift, with markings from above. Sometimes it was a kind gesture from a stranger or co-worker. Other times it was the awareness of the beauty of God's creation around me or the meaning of higher thoughts that flooded my mind.

After working in the factory for a couple of years, I was promoted and worked as a clerk in the office. I held this job for ten years. When business became slow at the factory and I was only working two or three days a week, I did not worry. Instead, I decided to look for a second job and worked as a nurses-aide on weekends. My husband was also promoted to a management position and this helped us financially, thus enabling us to save and buy our first home. Our lives continued to improve. God fulfilled my secret wishes, when a friend called one day and offered me a job as an assistant teacher at a pre-school. I was entering a new phase in life. I returned to teaching and served for twenty two years until my retirement in 2019.

Then one day, as I was painting my kitchen walls, a deluge of words rushed into my thoughts, to steer me in the right direction, and they were:

- Admire others and never be envious,
- My words and actions will speak for themselves,
- Simple foods are the healthiest,
- Speech, action, and the tone of a voice are very important to the human nature,
- Making a mistake is one thing, the other is accepting it,

- Have respect for everyone,
- The beauty of success is being able to handle and enjoy it,
- Time never waits for anyone but keeps on going,
- Not everything I see I should want, and not everything I want I should get,
- Work towards good health and peace of mind,
- Be independent and honor my responsibilities,
- Life is all about being satisfied and having peace of mind,
- Happiness is appreciating everything I worked for,
- Talking, understanding, and listening are essential ingredients in any kind of relationship,
- Understanding is the supernatural knowledge we all have but don't use,
- Delving into my bountiful, knowledgeable resources will enable me to achieve greater results,
- Criticisms are sometimes made with good intentions,
- When inspiration knocks on the door, use it,
- Share my thoughts but not my affection,
- Greatness comes from within,
- Be honest,
- Everyone will achieve achievements due to his or her own capabilities,
- Great thoughts comes from great minds,
- Use my thinking powers to the fullest,
- Do good things for the well-being of others,
- Some of us are born great, and some of us achieve greatness,
- New ideas will come from within like the twinkling of stars.

- My identity should be kept a secret which meant, that I don't want to be known. I *treasure* my quiet life.
- I am not what you see but what you don't see: meaning that anyone can see the physical me but no one can see the inner me.
- Within me is a genius guarded by invisible bodyguards meaning that God gave me wisdom from within and he is protecting me.
- I am a breath of fresh air entering a brand-new world. I came from a spiritual background to a spiritual awakening.

CHAPTER FOUR

Spiritual Awakening

YEARS LATER, I WAS CONTENT and very happy with my life. In some ways, I was like everyone else, working and taking care of myself and my family. There was also a deeper desire to serve God and give back some of what he had given me. I didn't realize that this wish would take me on a path, which led me to spiritual awakening. To me, this seemed impossible but I believe it was made possible because of what my Guru saw in me, a trove of hidden treasures buried deep within, waiting to be discovered.

My conviction to serve God, began to take root when I had an extraordinary visitor on Christmas Eve night, that same year. Everyone had gone to bed and I was watching a movie in my living room. During the commercials, I decorated our Christmas tree. After putting the finishing touches on the tree, I sat on the sofa, close to the television and continued watching the movie. A man dressed in white and wearing a gold crown, suddenly appeared in front of me smiling. I was dazed by his appearance, and for me time stood still. I felt frozen and stared at him in disbelief, as he continued to smile. He didn't say anything and his stay was very short. Surprisingly, I wasn't afraid and the next day, I was ecstatic just thinking about my unknown visitor. I believed this occurrence meant that a saintly being would appear in my life in the near future.

The following year on Christmas Eve night, I was doing the same thing, I did the year before.

I was watching television alone in my living room and during commercials, I was decorating the Christmas tree when I heard a thud, as if someone had thrown something. I immediately went to investigate and didn't see anything but as I continued to hang the decorations, something shiny on the floor caught my eye. Laying on the floor, next to the tree, was a flower, with gold-colored petals. I picked it up, and admired the dainty, shiny gold petals as I held it in my hand. It wasn't heavy and I was baffled at the sound, I had heard earlier. To me this was a blessing from God and my duty was to cherish it. From time to time, I look at it with affection and remembered the saintly visitor. I thank God for his continuous blessings.

One day, I was alone at home resting and I was thinking about God, the visitor and the flower, when two questions entered my mind, and they were, *was I a highly spiritual person several lifetimes ago? Will I rekindle my spiritual heritage?* I found the answers to these questions when my youngest daughter invited us to accompany her to a meditation center. In the beginning, I attended services whenever I felt like it but I was drawn to the preachers melodious singing, the rhythmic beat of the drums and the soul searching spiritual discussions. This environment was new to me and I didn't know anything about meditation or a Guru. I was astonished by how overwhelmingly calm and peaceful I felt, once I was there. This new found peace encouraged me to get initiated by my revered Guru.

Every Sunday morning, the meditation center was buzzing with activities. Groups of people were busy transforming the school's cafeteria for the spiritual service. Rugs were rolled out and vacuumed, clean, crisp sheets were spread over the rugs for attendees to sit and chairs were placed against a wall and at the back for the elderly. The stage was adorned with roses in two crystal vases and small lighted candles. A variety of scented flowers were used to form decorative shapes. Rose petals were placed neatly on both sides of the path, leading to the stage where my Guru's portrait rested on a sofa covered with an embroidered and sequined spread. As I looked at his portrait, the chambers in my heart automatically opened to embrace him and I wanted to keep him there as my savior and mentor. When this thought arose in my mind, I had hoped that, with sincere devotion, and meditation, he would carve out a pathway leading to his majestic abode.

Some people would prepare tasty vegetarian meals for lunch which was provided after the service. Then the cafeteria would be cleaned and there was never any shortage of helping hands. The people I met there, were helpful, kind and a mixture of different nationalities. If you're new, there were devotees who would greet, guide and made you feel comfortable. Their dedication to selfless service taught by my Guru was impressive and I was inspired to join them.

When I received initiation into divine knowledge, I had a vision. I saw myself sitting between two people. On my right was a man and on my left was a woman, both wore white garments. I was startled but after a few seconds, felt comfortable in their presence and sensed their benevolence towards me. I couldn't distinguish their faces but felt that they were connected to God. This was the first time I saw them and was curious to know who he was and where he came from, the word Guru entered my mind. All at once happiness and ease filled my heart, however, nothing was revealed to me about the woman.

As I continued meditating, I was blessed with another extraordinary vision. I saw my Guru and I walking. We walked for a while, and then a bridge materialized blocking our path. I was stunned for a few minutes and looked wide eyed at my Guru expecting him to say something, but instead he motioned me to cross over the bridge. Without any hesitation, I started walking and noticed many lighted lanterns hanging on both sides. Then at the end of the bridge, I was astonished to see Hindu Deities as little children, playing drums, singing and dancing. They were celebrating something momentous. Everyone was joyously clapping their hands and cheering in celebration.

Suddenly, I remembered my Guru and wanted him to be with me. I glanced backwards and he was still standing, on the other side. His gaze rested on me and soon after, he started walking in my direction. When he reached where I was, he placed his hand on my head. Two years later, I remembered this vision while meditating at the meditation center and then I realized what this vision was about. Crossing over that bridge symbolized my initiation into the spiritual path under the guidance of my Guru, without whom, it would not be possible.

Initially it was very difficult to concentrate in meditation. My thoughts would travel all over the universe but practice, patience, divine guidance and determination helped me to overcome my difficulties. I tried to meditate as often as possible, and the following Sunday, I went to the meditation center and was walking on the red carpet towards my revered Guru's alter. For the very first time, I felt a jolt of energy going through my body. That feeling was sudden and lasted for a few seconds but I pretended nothing happened.

From then on, every time, I closed my eyes to meditate, I had visions of my Guru and me. I as a little girl, holding on to his pinky finger and walking quietly with him. When I was having these spiritual visions, I didn't understand what they meant. Yet I was driven by the urge to write down everything I saw. Four years later, the answers came gradually as I progressed in meditation. I received a word here, a phrase there and I read my notes repeatedly. I put words and phrases together and tried to understand the meanings of the visions. It was like fixing a jig-saw puzzle.

Then one day, I was cleaning my apartment and I was thinking about my Guru. The thought crossed my mind that the visions were messages from my Guru. In the following visions, he outlined what would happen in the future on this journey and gave me exposure to his language. A language that I had to learn, in order to understand his messages.

CHAPTER FIVE

Visions from Meditation

Vision One

I WAS WALKING ALONE, AND as I was about to pass a large, old building, a woman suddenly appeared in front of me smiling. She opened a door and asked me to enter. I did and was greeted by the most magnificent sight. Several large exquisite chandeliers were hanging from the ceiling. Polished brown benches were laid out in straight lines. The floors and walls were immaculate. For a few seconds I was stunned at the beauty of this place as I tried to focus on my surroundings. I wanted to know, *why am I alone in this building?* Then I saw myself bowing my head and going down on my knees. Men wearing white garments, walked in a straight line towards me and as they passed by, each one of them placed their hand on my head, giving me their blessings. When I opened my eyes, I felt like I've won the lottery because these saintly beings gave me their blessings.

Vision Two

One Sunday morning, during a spiritual discourse, my Guru came and seemed to be in a jovial mood. Seeing him, made me so happy. He then walked towards me with his hand outstretched. I got up as usual, held on to his pinky finger, and we went next to the preacher's stage, listening and enjoying the devotional songs. Then, my Guru took something out from his pocket. It was a flag with outline shapes of all the different countries. He was twirling it in circles. Here my Guru was expressing that he represents people of all nationalities

Vision Three

I attended a meditation class led by the preachers at the meditation center. I closed my eyes, thinking about my Guru and tried to focus on their instructions, when suddenly an eye appeared in my vision. The eye was unbelievable, magnificent and unique. The eyebrows and eye lashes were grey, and I couldn't see the color of the iris. I was mesmerized and as I continued to focus on the eye, I felt waves of positive energy flowing into me. My confidence soared and my entire being felt elevated.

Early one morning, a month later, I was walking to the train station and looked up at the sky. I saw the face of an older person with eyes like the one, I saw in my vision before. The eyes were gentle, filled with compassion and my eyes became fixated on the apparition in the sky. I stopped walking and stood gazing at the face, until it slowly disappeared into the clouds. In that moment, I felt closer to God and knew that he was watching over me.

Vision Four

My Guru and I were having a serious conversation while we were walking one day in the park, and was distracted by the sounds of birds tweeting from a tree nearby. I randomly, looked up to see where the birds were and saw two open umbrellas descending upon us. A giant umbrella positioned itself over my Guru and he reached for it. The smaller one was hovering over me and I grabbed it. My understanding of this vision is that, by listening and following his instructions, I would always remain under his shelter and be guided through the harsh realities of life.

Vision Five

My Guru was pointing here and there as we walked on the pavement one afternoon. The weather was beautiful with a warm and gentle, breeze. He seemed to be teaching me something about our surroundings. That day we walked a couple of miles, when a wall appeared out of nowhere, blocking our path. I was frazzled a little bit and looked at my Guru for direction. Then a long ladder appeared instantly against the wall, and without any explanation, my Guru asked me to climb. I hesitated for a moment, then proceeded slowly. As I was climbing, I kept glancing back at him and he gestured for me to continue climbing to the top. Finally, I reached the top and stepped off onto a platform. I was astonished to find my Guru, already there, waiting for me. When he saw me, he began laughing at my bewildered expression, and immediately placed his hand on my head and gave me his blessings. Here my Guru was telling me, that under his guidance, I would be able to overcome all obstacles and obtain divine knowledge from him.

Vision Six

I was walking to the bus stop, and on my way, I saw a house with a long staircase leading down to the street level. I've never seen a building like this before and as I stood looking at it, a door opened and a dog ran out followed by a tall man. The dog was sniffing around while the man stood patiently waiting for him. The bus arrived and I found myself sitting next to the same man and his dog. He had the dog cradled on his lap and they were communicating in a language of their own. I didn't understand anything they were saying. The bus stopped and as I was about to exit, the man said "Hi! Later, it dawned on me that I had to learn to decipher my Guru's language.

Vision Seven

While I was meditating at the meditation center, I saw a woman walking towards me instead of my Guru. She came next to me, touched my hand, and beckoned me to follow her. We walked to the stage where the preachers were sitting and joined them in singing devotional songs. In this vision, my Guru was emphasizing that singing devotional songs would uplift my mind and that I should make the effort to learn to sing them.

Vision Eight

One Sunday, when the service ended, I saw my Guru swinging a metal pot with a long handle. Smoke was coming out from the bottom of the pot. Here my Guru was acknowledging our devotion and I understood that as the smoke rises, our consciousness was being elevated through spiritual discourses, meditation and prayers.

Vision Nine

I saw my Guru picking up pieces of wood from our driveway. My Guru was showing me that he would help me with the renovation of our basement apartment and he did. To save on the cost, I decided to paint the walls and ceilings, polish the window sills and the doors myself. I was working from 9am to 5pm but after dinner, I would go down to the basement and worked until mid-night every night. This continued until the basement was completed and my family was astonished at the volume of work I was doing. After the apartment was completed, I looked around and asked myself, how was I able to work nonstop and not feel tired? I realized it was because of my Guru immense grace. He gave me the energy and this taught me that hard work, dedication and determination will produce skillful results.

Vision Ten

One Sunday morning, I saw my Guru appearing at the meditation center all happy and cheerful. I noticed he was wearing a necklace with a heart pendant and on each side of the pendant there was an S. As usual, I held on to his pinky finger and walked with him towards the preachers on the stage. Then, he placed a necklace just like his around my neck. In giving me the necklace, I believed it signifies him imparting his treasures of divine knowledge to me through meditation.

Vision Eleven

I was in deep meditation one day and saw my Guru and I walking. This day we walked, stopped, walked again, while glancing at all the buildings as we pass them. He seemed to be describing something and as we continued on our leisurely walk, we approached a huge iron gate. Then, I noticed that he was deliberately walking at a slower pace. I was ahead of him and slowed down, with the thought that he would catch up with me. The gate opened suddenly, and I entered thinking that he was behind me. There was a path leading to the front of a huge building and as I walked, I remembered my Guru and turned around to see if he was behind me. He wasn't and I began to look for him in every direction, trying to get a glimpse of him. Guru was nowhere to be seen and I was worried because he didn't say anything to me about leaving. This was not like him and I couldn't believe that he would just leave. I felt completely lost without him. I asked myself, why am I here and wondered who was living in the building. As I approached the front entrance, the door opened suddenly, which made me think that someone was expecting me. I entered and saw Lord Rama standing. This vision meant that my Guru would take the form of Lord Rama to show me the truth through meditation.

Vision Twelve

A man wearing a turban, and riding a buffalo approached me and took me for a ride. He didn't say a word and after a while brought me back to where I was, and quickly disappeared in the horizon. I believed that he was a saint.

Vision Thirteen

Early one morning, I had a vision of myself sitting on an elephant with my Guru walking beside me. Here my Guru was using the elephant to show me an example of courage, strength and endurance.

CHAPTER SIX

Meditation Awakened My Love For God

MY LOVE FOR GOD GREW after I began meditating and a small flame was lit in my heart. The more I meditated and purified my heart and mind, that flame grew bigger and bigger. This strong feeling followed me like a shadow everywhere. I was blown away by this miraculous closeness, I felt with our heavenly Father. He was on my mind all the time and I wanted to be in his sanctuary where I felt safe, and secured. Here I was experiencing the purest emotion in my life, *love* for God. It made me feel sacred and special and I wanted to hold on to it for as long as possible. My other relationships, held an emptiness in comparison to my feelings and I had to free myself from all my social ties. I lost interest in people that I liked and known for many years. Of course, they were upset with me and I was sorry for hurting them but I couldn't explain this change in my behavior. I wanted to be alone, to concentrate and dedicate myself in devotion. In reality, I knew this opportunity was grand, it wasn't something ordinary, it was a rare gem among gems.

Then my Guru laid out the many benefits of meditating under his supreme guidance. He gave me the tool which is meditation and guidelines to follow. Meditation became an important part of my daily routine, and I began meditating early in the morning, late at night and in my spare time. It opened several doors for me and I saw visions of my future and my Guru. I wrote poems and stories. I saw colors I've never seen before, flowers and roses of all varieties and most important, I saw light. For me a new path became accessible and I was sent immediately into the unknown, where I found peace, truth, happiness, and sincerity. Meditation changed me, my way of living and my way of thinking. It opened the doors to receiving answers from the Divine. For me, this connection is deeper than prayers. I was captivated and visions of my Guru's teachings filled each session. We were always together and after I meditated, I would feel peaceful and calm.

Whenever I meditated, I saw myself as a very young child, walking with my Guru while holding on to his pinky finger. Years later, I remembered this and reflected on its meaning, then in January 2017, I realized what he was trying to tell me. He was telling me that my education in spiritual knowledge was that of an infant. For me to learn about his world, I had to start from the ABC's of spirituality which I discovered through meditation.

God's language is mysterious and difficult to understand. However, in meditation, I received the inspiration to decipher the meaning of his divine messages. I am always in awe of my Guru's compassionate lessons, when I figure out the meaning of a sentence or a phrase of his. Instantly, I would feel the deepest gratitude towards him and a pure sensation spreading through my being.

My Guru brought good fortune, respect, creativity, knowledge, and positive energy into my life. I am always so appreciative to God and my Guru for uncovering an abundance of possibilities within me. One day, while I was listening to devotional songs which I enjoy, a bunch of words just dropped in my thoughts and they were: *Father you inspire me to do the unattainable every moment of my life.* After I meditated at night, sometimes new ideas would invade my sleep in the early morning hours. I would have to get out of bed and write them down. After I did this, I would go back into bed and be able to sleep peacefully. Everything that I wrote, turned out to be another lesson learned from him. Here, I learned that dedication and making sacrifices are key ingredients to elevating myself.

With his presence and energy always around me, everything I worked on, be it at work or home was completed with the end results always surprising me. I was humbled and in disbelief by the magnitude of my Guru's divinity. With humility, I received his divine grace and guidance, pointing me towards divine knowledge. Many times my Guru would toss phrases that instantly landed in my mind but the answers came later. Here are a few examples:

> *I found peace and tranquility within myself.* I learned that one should respond to difficult situations with a calm and balanced mind. Instead of reacting, one should remain composed.

The impossible became possibilities. For me seeing my Guru as Lord Rama, hearing that voice from within, my feelings for God and my Guru, made me realize that with my Guru, even the impossible could become possible. These were all new and empowering to me.

Gradually my thinking powers changed and a new personality emerged. In many of my visions, we walked along the Brighton Beach shoreline, which looked like a beautiful painting with rippling ocean waves, vibrant green sea weeds and sand dotted with sea shells. I developed a habit of walking and admiring anything that caught my interest and felt a deeper enjoyment for nature.

Meditation gave me the one-of-a-kind experiences. My inner world exploded and I saw saintly beings giving me their blessings graciously.

Meditation purified my soul and allowed me to discover the purity of God. Meditation worked like a cleansing agent, removing the rust from my inner and outer worlds.

God became my Guru and I became the symbol of God. My Guru would lead me to achieve the highest knowledge, God.

I saw myself as a very young child lying at God's feet in a deep sleep. My Guru awakened my thirst to know myself and love God. He knew that I was ready.

In my visions, my Guru worked on both my personal and work life. One by one he guided me to improve my character flaws and planted seeds of humility, wisdom, love for everyone and the freedom to express myself. Many times, when I had the opportunity to give a speech, my Guru would intervene unexpectedly. I was always astounded by how effortlessly the words flowed without much preparation from me. I was able to speak with confidence. Under the shelter of my Perfect Master, positive thoughts ushered in and I became the pen following his direction.

Meditation under the guidance of my Guru slowly transported me on the path of divine wisdom. This whole experience feels like an impossible dream. I am still in shock and cannot describe my feelings. When I think of my Guru, I feel like anointing his feet for the rest of my life, and I want him to know that the hours he spent teaching me would never go wasted. He gave me a peek into his world and I idolize him for it.

CHAPTER SEVEN

My Beloved Guru

I COULDN'T BELIEVE THAT SOMEONE could be physically in another country, so far away and know so much about me. My Guru knew more about me than I knew about myself. I've never met him in person and got to know him very well, only in meditation. I saw pictures of him and I couldn't believe that this God like personality, would use his precious time to teach me. For me, he is the king of spiritual knowledge. He used visions to teach me instead of books. How could this be? Impossible I would say but true. He is a great magician and with him, everything is possible. Whenever I meditated, I saw us walking with him pointing here and there. We were looking all around admiring and observing our surroundings. I would write whatever I saw in meditation and at night read the written materials. I knew that I on my own couldn't write like this. He awakened my curiosity to discover myself and showed me on several occasions my capabilities. I didn't know then that this Majestic Icon, was the source tapping into my thoughts with divine knowledge. Now I know that it was him all along. Tears well up in my eyes when I remember this Divine Being and his extraordinary generosity. I know that I cannot repay him but the least I can do is write this story and allow others to know him. I am humbled by his never ending lessons.

Before I embarked on this journey, I prayed whenever I felt like praying and never imagined that one day, my Guru would give me the opportunity to fulfill my highest purpose. I've always tried to do the right things in my life and whenever I've made a mistake, I immediately acknowledged it, prayed and asked God for forgiveness. I am thankful, that God showered his blessings on me and I was sent on a mission to attain spiritual knowledge. I spent a number of years not knowing what was in store for me. I was scared but my trust in God never wavered because I knew that he would guide me on the right path. I thank God for giving me the privilege to experience the impossible under his supervision and despite the multitude of uncertainties in my mind, I arrived in the shelter of my Guru.

My Guru is my passport into the spiritual world, and he is my fountain of divine knowledge. The doors of awareness opened and I saw light everywhere. I learned how to be righteous and how to think positively. In my limited mind, he was beyond brilliant. I worked towards happiness, good health and peace in my everyday life. As he continued to infuse realization into my mind, a new personality emerged, and a new character came into existence. I became more compassionate with my family and the people I knew. With his encouragement, guidance, and divine energy floating around me, I was able to accomplish peace of mind, and serenity.

He visited me regularly in visions especially while meditating at the meditation center. With his presence and enlightened energy in my life everything was attainable and I was free from any stress. He taught me with words raining down from above, with visions in meditation and in dreams. His persona was that of a jovial person, and he was fun to be with. He loved to sing, dance and was also an avid story teller. We were always walking, observing, and looking at everything. Sometimes he threw flowers joyfully on his devotees and other times he was in deep contemplation.

My Guru brilliantly worked miracles with my mind and geared me towards creativity and self-reliance. It began many years ago with the spontaneous urge to read, write, design and create. Under his supervision, my imagination grew wings and soared. In my visions, I was a little girl, obedient and eager to learn. I listened enthusiastically and willingly followed his instructions. I saw myself quietly doing my chores and did a little bit more than was expected of me. His grace often reached beyond my visions and into my everyday life to help me move forward and overcome every obstacle. He encouraged me to keep learning. I felt like I was in a boot camp with my Guru observing, grasping, memorizing, emulating his behavior and learning new skills. He treated me like I was an unusual piece of diamond and his job was to polish me around the edges and shape me into a one of a kind piece.

At work, I developed the ability to create art lessons and sew pretend play costumes. At home, I started making my own Christmas tree decorations. I knew how to use a sewing machine but never considered sewing anything for the class room before, yet I found myself sewing skillfully. Then I and a group of teachers joined an organization and we crocheted winter baby hats, scarves and blankets for charity. I didn't know how to crochet well, all I knew was the first step, making chains. A colleague demonstrated additional steps and I was surprised how quickly I mastered it. Not only did my Guru give me the opportunities to learn and display my ability, he also blessed me with recognition from others who admired my work. I felt indebted to my Guru because of my new God given skills and I considered him to be my solid rock. I knew I couldn't succeed in doing these projects on my own and I will always treasure the memories of him helping me.

One Sunday, I was in deep meditation and I saw myself looking, and observing my Guru as he was standing nearby. On the surface he looked like a man but from time to time, I saw glimpses of his immense compassion and infinite wisdom. My Guru has charisma and charm. He is funny when he is happy. He showed me repeatedly his love for all people. My Guru sees the potential in all beings and is here to elevate everyone unconditionally. He never discriminates and loves to give second chances or even third. He treats everyone equally and fairly. A spiritual being of his caliber is one in a million. I know because of what he has done for me, my family and many others.

At the meditation center the preachers sang devotional songs in Hindi and Punjabi followed by the English translation. Listening and singing devotional songs is one of my favorite things to do. It makes me happy and I feel closer to God. I wanted to learn to sing some of the songs so badly but the pronunciation was a challenge for me until I learned to unscramble the sounds. Most importantly, I am fascinated by the poetic meanings which caught my attention like an insect in a spider's web. I was helped by my Guru when he graced me with his love and presence at the meditation center. Eventually the pronunciation of the words came naturally, as if I knew the language and now I can sing the choruses of many devotional songs. Here my Guru was showing me that with a little help from him and efforts of my own, I could overcome any challenge.

I didn't know that soon after, I would experience his boundless grace during a prayer meeting service. A group of people were singing hymns, and I joined them. As I was singing, I felt a gentle touch on my back, and my voice changed and soared above everyone else's. I knew that voice wasn't mine, and I was amazed how professional it sounded. The voice was beautiful and booming. I was stunned at my Guru's revelation, and later, the people gathered around me, to express their admiration. My Guru elevated my confidence that day and I felt secured under his guidance. This practical experience of his grace, was just the beginning. He seemed to be reassuring me that my sincerity and devotion on this path would act like a strong potion that will push me to do extraordinary things beyond my imagination.

He laid the foundation for my spiritual education to facilitate the expansion of my consciousness. He taught me to be my own person, my perspective changed, and I became a dreamer with aspiration. I tried my very best to gain his respect and not to disappoint him. He lifted me up when I was falling and gave me hope when I needed it the most. He instilled higher values in me, and slowly but surely, I learned many priceless lessons from him. As a teacher, he was rigorous and didn't spoil me.

Years later, I began to understand that being within my Guru's sphere of influence enhanced my abilities. He continuously showed me, what I was capable of doing and that I can work independently. At the same time, he was demonstrating to me that I am important and my thoughts are also important. I realized now, that everything was manageable only because of his intervention in my life.

My Guru's holistic teachings also gave me greater insight into my well-being. Through the tool of meditation, my mind gained clarity regarding every aspect of my life. The positive energy that I gathered in meditation brought a glow to my skin and luster to my hair. Without a reason, my love of mangoes, pineapples and potatoes changed and suddenly I had no desire to eat them. Then a few months later, I was diagnosed with border line diabetes but my body had already given me a signal. I paid close attention to what I consumed and lost twenty pounds. I was surprised by how healthy I felt.

I was never a good dancer. Whenever I tried to dance, my body was too stiff and wouldn't co-operate. Then one day, I felt like dancing. I got up and started dancing. My arms and body's co-ordination was a surprise to me. I saw myself dancing with skill and gracefulness. I was shocked to realize that I could dance. All I needed was practice, so I decided to use dancing as a form of exercise and began dancing every night. My body isn't stiff anymore, in fact, it is more flexible all because of dancing.

Whenever I saw my Guru while meditating, he used himself as an example to teach me about attitude. I've never seen him angry or upset when he was teaching me. Even though he was constantly active, he was always calm and patient. Seeing this, I was motivated to follow his example and changed my behavior.

Usually in my visions, I saw myself as a little girl holding on to his pinky finger and walking with him. As I progressed spiritually, it was reflected in my appearance and I saw myself looking older. I often saw him giving me errands and would observe, how I followed through from afar. He would commend my achievements whole heartedly by touching my head and I knew that he was giving me his blessings. Knowing this inspired me, to work on more projects in the classroom, while encouraging the children to participate. In his presence everything was orderly and harmonious. I worked at replicating this in my surroundings by keeping everything neat and clean.

I was learning so much from him and I felt like my intelligence level was rising bit by bit. I was not the only one who benefited. I also witnessed our new ideas being implemented in the other classrooms. When they were brought to life, they were admired by many and others were motivated. I noticed that his presence in my life made a difference with the children, be it in their speech, fine motor skills or art activities. One day, I was working in a classroom with three year old children and I was the closing teacher. Most of the children were picked up except for one boy. I gave him large plastic blocks to play with while waiting for his parents. Instead of building a tower like he did before, he placed the blocks horizontally across the room and said that he built a bridge. He never did this before even though he had access to the blocks every day. When his parents came to pick him up, they were impressed and so was I.

This is just one example of the spontaneous bursts of creativity that would occur periodically at work. At home, I was consumed by the unrelenting urge to write and words flowed into my mind like rivulets rushing to reach their destination. I meditated all the time and because of this, I felt empowered and fulfilled. It was as if I was being molded by the technique of a master sculptor which required only my surrender. I grew up as a farmer's daughter in Guyana, worked hard and got accepted to a nursing program in England. However, my mother became ill and asked me to stay. Within six months she died and so did my dream of becoming a nurse. New dreams emerged when my Guru came into my life, this time, with the assurance of completion under his supervision. With each lesson, vision or situation, he expertly influenced my thinking to produce change in me. I had a lot to learn and I marveled at his simple but profound lessons. He knew the capacity of my intelligence and tailored his approach to have the greatest impact. It is because of his grace, I found myself in the company of the highest truth, embodied by my Guru and divine avatars. To my astonishment, my Guru planned the grandest intervention to help me evolve. During this time, my life revolved around the companionship of my Guru, Lord Rama, and Lord Ganesh. When I least expected it, one of them would appear in my visions to begin a new chapter in my evolution.

These are the visions, and my interpretations about the future of my journey that resonated deeply.

- I saw my Guru holding a big circular key ring. I was standing with a group of people, and he threw the key ring towards us. It landed around my neck. *He gave me the keys to eternal wisdom.*

- I saw myself wearing a gown and my Guru placed a graduation cap on my head. *I was ready to be blessed with the practical realization of God.*

- One day I saw my Guru appearing all excited, with his arms outstretched, and swung me around. *Gaining divine intelligence would revolve around him.*

- I saw my Guru anointing my head and he said, *go show them what you can do, so that through you, they can learn about me.*

- I saw my Guru and me holding a large piece of paper and people were flocking in large numbers to read what was written on it. *He would give me inspiration to share with others.*

- I saw my Guru and I wearing crowns meaning that, *I would gain eternal knowledge from him.*

- I saw my Guru knocking on doors which meant that, continued devotion and meditation would *open the doors to higher consciousness.*

- I saw myself touching my Guru and Lord Ram's feet *in gratitude and supplication.*

- I saw myself becoming a universal flag and for me this meant that, *my Guru's message is global.*

- I saw the bud of a yellow rose and a brightly lit light bulb and then the words, bask in the glory of being me entered my mind, which meant, that*, my Guru gave me the technique to immerse myself in the wealth of sacred inner light, which meditation revealed.*

CHAPTER EIGHT

Insights

HERE, THIS PERFECT SPIRITUAL MASTER, my Guru, was imparting profound insight to me. He worked like a master gardener to extract the weeds and replaced them with fragrant flowering plants. With unrelenting patience, my Guru worked with me to embed the following philosophies of life.

Be independent,
Hold on to my family,
Focus on treating everyone fair,
Be sincere to everyone,
Surround myself with people who genuinely care,
Learn from my mistakes and try not to repeat them,
Listen carefully to everyone,
Speak the truth or not speak at all,
Look at strangers from afar,

Understand that everyone is entitled to his or her own opinion,

Treat everyone with dignity and respect,

Enjoy nature,

Use a soft tone whenever I speak,

Mediate conflict,

Embrace success with dignity and poise,

Always maintain stability in my daily life,

Make sacrifices if I have to,

Help as much as I can,

Never hate or be jealous of anyone because anger, hate and jealously can only destroy me,

Do not judge anyone,

That goodness and truth will always prevail.

I practiced what he taught me and my outlook on life changed for the better. I stopped worrying over trivial matters. I was a worrier before and instead of worrying, I resort to meditation which generates calm and clarity in my mind. The rough patches that life inevitably offers on and off became manageable.

One day, I was looking at my youngest grandson Sam and was thinking to myself that he looked thin and weak. Later that day when I meditated, I saw my Guru giving an old fashioned door key to Sam. I knew then that my Guru would help Sam and I felt an overwhelming gratitude at his quick response to my worry, which immediately put my mind at ease. His patience and tolerance with me was unbelievable. He taught me to pay attention to all the positive aspects of my daily life and no matter how much negativity I encountered, I should cultivate an optimistic outlook. This way of thinking was the remedy for my depressive state of mind. He wanted me to look at everyday things with greater awareness and my interest in my daily activities was so much better than before. Upon surrendering fully to his logic about my life, I gained confidence and never looked back.

I pushed myself to meditate more and more, because I wanted to see my Guru and was always curious to find out what was next in our adventure. The beautiful melody of birds chirping and sunbeams streaming into my room in the morning, made me feel like my Guru was giving me a special wake up call. I felt honored and this set the tone for my day. I found that keeping my mind constantly on God and my Guru while doing my chores, gave me inexhaustible energy. I worked non-stop for hours, and my everyday duties were accomplished to an extent that I was shocked. He transmitted to me a keen love and appreciation for nature. As we cruised along on our walks, I discovered beauty and took the time to admire the unique quality each tree and flower possessed. I had not felt this kind of wonder since my childhood in Guyana.

My Guru always surprised me with his brilliant creative ideas to keep the children in my class room engaged and content. Every time, he taught me something new, my Guru would use a different approach and I felt that I was an instrument working under his supervision. I realized that the more I meditated with devotion, I was able to gather more positive energy which influenced my work performance. New ideas flowed spontaneously and I saw how small changes can have a huge impact on the children which worked wonders with their short attention span.

Eventually, the precious visions stopped, even though I continued meditating and was replaced with something unexpected. I had the strongest urge to write, and words flowed into my mind, like a stream of running water. I was obsessed with writing and during this time, I lost my appetite and didn't care about food. I seemed to be fasting without realizing it. I felt driven to write and was consumed with a conviction that I had to do this. I wrote in the trains, at home, during my lunch hour and at the meditation center. At the end of the day, I had several pieces of paper stuffed in my pants pocket. At night, I would read them and admired the presentation of the words and phrases. After so many years, I marveled as to why again and what was the reason? I had a very strong feeling that the writings would lead me to something remarkable. With this in mind, I continued passionately on my writing mission which materialized because of my Guru. I couldn't believe how fortunate I was and my faith in my Guru deepened. This was when I decided passionately, that whatever challenges he offered me, I would accept them willingly and try my very best to fulfill his expectations. Disappointing him was never in my mind. Several times, I saw him placing his hand on my head and I knew that he was giving me his blessings. This act of his meant everything to me then and now. I considered it to be priceless.

I've always admired people who give others a chance to shine. My Guru pushes his devotees and allows them to reach their full potential. Can I ever thank him enough? *No never.* My affection and gratitude for him grew in size from a hill to a mountain range. My Guru laid down the foundation for my personal growth, which helped me to change my way of thinking. He instilled in me the determination to rise above my limitations.

Be myself,
Strive toward happiness and good health,
Enjoy peaceful atmospheres.
Render help to anyone and everyone.
Use dialogue to solve a problem.
Talk less and do more.
Climb the spiritual ladder without looking back.

CHAPTER NINE

Poems /Stories

MY CONFIDENCE WAS AT A new high, when words and phrases rained down from above to create mini poems and children stories. These stories were written quickly, and I was amazed how easily they were formed in my mind. Even though they are simple, they represented the grandeur of my Guru's presence and energy in my life. When I completed the stories and reviewed them, I caught glimpses of my Guru's messages and his eternal wisdom. I realized that everything was in the hands of my beholder, my Guru. Without him, I couldn't write or complete the stories and now whenever I read them, the memories of his presence would return, as if it was yesterday.

This Big, Old House

This big, old house, a hundred years old,
Built by a captain, a seafaring man.

He built a cabin on top of the roof
To see all the ships that came to port

The Snow

Oh! The snow, the snow,
So pure, so innocent,
Year after year she returns,
Like an obedient child,
To decorate the landscape with her white blanket.

That Long, Long Road

That long, long road,
That long, long road,
There's no end to that long, long road,
A road paved with gold, diamonds, and rubies,
Has charms and affection for everyone to experience.

David and the White Elephant

David loves to go hunting with his father in the woods. One day as they were hunting, he heard a sound in the bushes and went to investigate. Lying on the ground and covered with dirt was an elephant. As he went closer, the elephant said to him, *please help me. I am starving. I need food and water.* David went in search of his father and brought him to see the elephant. David's father was a kindhearted person and instantly agreed to help the elephant. They fed the elephant and took care of all his needs. After three months, the elephant regained his strength and was able to fend for himself but the thought of leaving, troubled him.

He liked David and his father. He didn't want to leave. When David saw that the elephant was unhappy, he knew why, and took the elephant to stay on their farm.

Then the elephant said to David, *I have one more request. I need a bath.* David willingly gave him a bath and was surprised to discover that the elephant was no ordinary elephant. He was young, beautiful and could do tricks. David hugged him, while thinking, that this elephant could live with them forever. Good deeds will always be remembered by those who receive them.

Sam

Sam loved the outdoors and was always attracted to the birds, squirrels and the plants in his grandpa's small vegetable garden. He would follow the birds and squirrels and helped with planting the vegetables. Occasionally, he watered the plants and usually poured water on himself. Sam loved to go fishing with his father and brother. Feeding and petting the animals at the petting zoo, was always an exciting adventure, which made him very happy. He would stay in the driveway, with a big smile on his face and looked at the people passing by. Sam made friends easily and the neighbor's cats were his pets. He gave them treats every day.

When he was six years old, his grandpa bought him a bike and taught him how to ride it. Within a month, Sam was riding his bike, holding on with one hand and calling on his grandpa to look at him. Grandpa would give him an encouraging smile. Whenever Sam fell off his bike, Grandpa would rush to pick him up, but Sam would get up quickly, saying that he was okay, and would continue to ride his bike. Sam proved to be tougher than Grandpa thought.

Each year, during the winter months, he couldn't wait for the warm spring and hot summer days to return. Well, it was summer again, and after school, Sam would rush home, opened the door, threw his bag on the floor, and rushed to join his friends at the park. His love for the outdoors seemed to be growing more and more as he gets older.

The Doghouse

Ben and his dog lived alone, and when he went to work, the dog was left at home all day. The dog ate, slept, and waited for Ben to return home. After a while the dog felt lonely and was very unhappy. Ben sensed that his dog was unhappy but didn't know what to do. He couldn't bear to see him so sad and after much thinking decided to build his dog a big, spacious doghouse. Ben furnished the doghouse with all sorts of toys and every morning, he took the dog and left him there for the day. He went to work, knowing that the dog would be busy playing with the toys and in the afternoons, Ben took his dog for long walks in the parks and around the neighborhood. At last the dog seemed happy and content. There are so many ways to create happiness.

The Mirror

The children in this classroom loved to play dress-up and used the mirror quite often. This mirror meant a lot to them, especially to one little girl in particular. Every morning, she would look in the mirror before she had her breakfast.

The mirror was always spotless, but this day, a little boy was playing with his toy car, and pretended the mirror was a field. He pushed his car in all directions and left tire marks all over the mirror. Efforts to clean the tire marks were unsuccessful but despite the imperfections, the children continued to use the mirror more so than before. New costumes were introduced in the classroom and dressing up became a popular activity with the children. I found that innocent minds are unreceptive to judging imperfections.

Franklin and the Boy Next Door

Franklin the cat enjoyed Tom's company, a six-year-old boy who lived in the building next door. Whenever, Tom was outdoors the cat would join him. Tom had a small yellow chair, and when he was tired of running around, he would sit on the chair to rest. Franklin would jump on his lap, and Tom frequently stroked his head, and showered him with tender loving care. Franklin was happy with this little boy as his friend.

Then Franklin's family decided to go away for three months, and Tom was devastated when he heard the news. Tom gave Franklin a treat every day until it was time for him to leave. After Franklin left, Tom kept himself busy with his classroom assignments, but Franklin was always on his mind. Franklin also missed Tom. He was counting the days and months, and finally it was time to return home. Franklin was happy and couldn't wait to see Tom. When Tom heard the good news, he sat on his yellow chair with a brand-new book, waiting for Franklin. A car stopped, and Franklin jumped out and ran towards Tom. Tom gave him a hug, and with Franklin curled snuggly on his lap, read him a story. Franklin soon fell into a deep sleep, happy to be with his friend again.

Farmer Joe

Farmer Joe lived on a farm with his pet monkey, named Peter. A friend who migrated to another country had given the monkey to him. Farmer Joe promised his friend that he would take good care of Peter. He treated Peter very well and selected the best fruits for his meals.

Unknown to Farmer Joe, Peter would sneak out of the house every night and went to the other farms in the neighborhood. He ate, destroyed some of the fruits and broke several branches from the trees. When the farmers saw the destruction in the mornings, they were angry and wanted to know who would do such a thing. Secretly, they decided to take turns watching over the farms at night. Then one night, the farmers heard a noise among the fruit trees, and silently went to investigate. They threw a net and Peter was caught. Farmer Joe was astonished and very upset with Peter. He didn't want to punish him. After all, he had promised his friend that he would take good care of him but he was afraid that Peter might be tempted to steal again.

Peter felt terrible when he saw how distressed Farmer Joe was and felt remorse for what he had done. Shamefacedly, he approached Farmer Joe, and promised him that he would never steal again. Peter decided to repay the farmers by working with them on their farms, and the farmers happily forgave him.

My Brother's Belt

My brother was the eldest and my only brother. He had six sisters including me. My brother and I were calm, soft-spoken people. We were like our mom, but when we were upset, we could be loud. I always imagined my brother wearing a belt with all of us hanging on it—my mom, dad, sisters, and me. When he got married, his wife joined us; and when his children came along, eight boys, they were placed next to his wife on the belt. My brother wore that belt his whole life, enjoying all the perks that came with being the only son and brother. His nickname was King.

My brother loved to eat, and when he was older, he couldn't control his diet. I saw that belt moving from one direction to the next, with all of us running to support and help him. He was a diabetic and eventually lost both legs. My brother had a good sense of humor and made us laugh all the time. Sometimes he took advantage of that belt and knew that whenever he shook his belt, we were all there to help him. We understood his intentions and didn't mind at all. We pampered him and he knew how we felt about him. We didn't use words, but there was a mutual understanding among us. We looked at one another and felt that strong bond that exists between a brother and his sisters.

After his wife died, that belt was drawn closer and tighter. We had a stronger and more solid relationship with my brother. A couple of years later, my brother was really sick, and we knew he was going to die. I saw that imaginary belt slipping away and felt helpless. I wanted to comfort him and tell him how much we loved him. I was crying hysterically, and as I looked at him, these words rushed into my mind.

Feelings

I have a secret to tell you.
I love you very much.

VR

I will never forget you,
So don't you worry, my dear brother
Go rest in peace.

When my brother was really sick, I was worried and couldn't sleep. I closed my eyes trying to fall asleep, and I had a vision. My Guru came, and we walked toward a fenced-in area. We looked below from where we were standing and everything looked dirty and then he took me somewhere else. When I looked down, everything looked beautiful and clean. I knew then that my brother would be in a better place when he passed. This vision consoled me and helped me to move on.

The Brown Door

This solid brown door, intricately designed,
With a mixture of browns and etchings of gold,
The designs were impressive, and caught my attention,
As I looked at the door, memories of my brother came,
Swirling in my mind of how strong he was.

"Feelings" and "The Brown Door" are dedicated to my dearest and only brother who made me laugh whenever I visited him.

Father

As long as I can remember, every afternoon in the summer, my father and I went somewhere. We never stayed in the house, especially if the weather was nice. We spent the afternoons at the parks, the boardwalk, or the beach.

He gave me the freedom to meet new friends, explore with sand toys, go up and down the slides, run, jump, climb, swim, and play ball. Under his watchful eyes, I felt safe. As the years went by, father taught me to be independent. Instead of holding my hand when we walked, I found myself walking beside him. Our walks became learning sessions, and father was my teacher. In my eyes he was a scholar and my security blanket.

Then as I got older, father asked me to walk in front of him. He stayed behind but was encouraging me to do things on my own. That night I had a dream. I saw a tall ladder, and father asked me to climb. Without hesitation, I climbed, and he kept repeating the words "keep going." I was nervous and a little bit scared. When I reached the top, I thought, *what's next?* But to my astonishment, he was already there and with a broad smile complimented me.

That dream made me realize how important a father is and my feelings for him increased a hundred times. Every day, I felt like it was my duty to shower him with love and respect as often as possible.

This story is dedicated to my parents, who worked tirelessly and made an enormous amount of sacrifices to educate me and my siblings. They were strict but loving and provided very well for us. There was always an abundance of fresh fruits, vegetables, and a variety of cooked meals.

The Mango Tree

Matt lived at home with his parents, and their home was surrounded by fruit trees. He helped his parents maintain the trees and enjoyed picking the ripe fruits and eating them. One day, he asked his parents to plant a mango tree.

He loved mangoes, and for his birthday, his parents planted a mango tree as a surprise gift for Matt. He was delighted with his gift. With care, the tree grew big and strong with many branches.

It was mango season, and Matt hoped that he would pick mangoes from his very own tree. The tree was filled with flowers, and Matt kept looking and looking for mangoes. The mango season was near ending, and Matt was worried. He thought something was wrong with the tree, but then one day, while he was eating his lunch, there was a basket filled with ripe mangoes on the table. He was curious and wanted to know where the mangoes came from. He went under his mango tree, looking for mangoes, and to his surprise, he saw several bunches of mangoes hidden among the green leaves. He was delighted and decided to share his own mangoes with his family and friends.

Grandma's Little Helper

Sam was a curious and daring seven year old boy. He often got in trouble with his mother and brother. He could be very challenging at times, but despite all these qualities, Sam would help his Grandma with chores. He swept the driveway and bought milk or juice from the grocery store.

When the bedroom door was locked and Grandma couldn't find the key to unlock the door, Sam knew how to open the door with a steak knife. He was always given a treat after he completed his chores, or Grandma would cook his favorite meal. This made Sam very happy. Sometimes, he puts on a show for others, without thinking of the consequences and Grandma would defend him. When he was upset or sad, Grandma was always there to soothe and comfort him.

Sam Loves Grandpa

Sam and his parents lived with his grandparents. He was the youngest of six grandchildren. Everyone loved him and treated him with kindness. He loved his brother, his cousins and his Grandpa. Grandpa called him "Sammy Boy."

Then his parents moved. The new apartment was ten minutes away from Grandpa's house, and Sam was having a hard time, because his Grandpa wasn't there. Late at night, Sam would call, asking for Grandpa but Grandpa would be asleep by then, and Sam would leave a message for him. His message was, *I miss you, and I love you.* Then one night, Sam told his mom that he knew why he wasn't happy. He told her that he missed his Grandpa.

When Grandpa heard of Sam's dilemma, he decided to spend three afternoons a week with Sam, but that wasn't enough for Sam. He wanted to be with Grandpa every day. When the middle-floor apartment in Grandpa's house was vacated, Sam with his family happily moved in. *Love conquers.*

The Crossing Guard

Nell was ten years old and was fearful of crossing busy streets and roads. On school days, she was happy to see the crossing guard in the mornings and afternoons. Seeing the crossing guard gives her a sense of security, and her fear would disappear. One Friday morning, she was late for school, and as she was approaching the street, she wondered whether the crossing guard was there. The crossing guard wasn't there. Afraid to cross, Nell thought of asking someone to help her. She looked around but didn't see anyone. She was getting worried, and then something phenomenal happened. Suddenly there was a gust of wind. It blew a one-gallon plastic bottle into the center of the road. Looking at the bottle gave her an idea. She pretended the bottle was the crossing guard and quickly crossed the street safely. That day she realized how important the crossing guard was.

From then on, every morning she waved to the crossing guard, who would acknowledge her with a big smile. Nell's fear of crossing streets and roads slowly disappeared. She became an advocate to those who were afraid to cross streets and roads in her classroom.

CHAPTER TEN

Guru's Surprise

MY GURU HAD A SPECIAL surprise for me at the meditation center one Sunday. When I closed my eyes, I saw my Guru with a man standing beside him. The man was tall, blue and radiant. As usual, my Guru came next to me with his hand outstretched. I held on to his pinky finger and walked with him toward the preachers on stage. I wanted to know who the man was. Just as I was thinking about him, two words sprung from within, *Lord Rama*. My Guru didn't mention anything previously about Lord Rama. Although, I was aware of their identity in my visions, I didn't fully grasp that God's representatives were my teachers. My Guru showed me, myself as an innocent child with complete surrender. This was his way to make my mind receptive and this was how I learned.

From here on, whenever I meditated, I saw my Guru and Lord Rama, and then I saw more and more of Lord Rama and less and less of my Guru. Then one Sunday, I was meditating and saw myself filled with adoration and holding on to one of my Guru's legs. He was laughing and said to Lord Rama, *look what she is doing*. Over the next few weeks, I experienced visions which resonated deeply and gave me a glimpse into my future. After weeks of seeing my Guru and Lord Rama together at the meditation center, I began to see only Lord Rama who continued to teach me important lessons about humanity. In the Hindu tradition, Lord Rama is a divine avatar who personifies the characteristic of an ideal person.

At various stages in my life, my Guru manifested in different forms to illuminate challenging situations and provide guidance to ultimately lead me to a higher understanding. He taught me through his example and I often observed that when my Guru was solving a problem, he was silent and in deep contemplation. I benefited greatly by trying to emulate his behavior especially when facing difficulties.

One morning, I was meditating at home and saw my Guru and I walking. After sometime, a huge iron gate appeared in front of us. I looked at my Guru, expecting him to say something. He was silent but with his hand, he signaled that I should walk in front of him. I did so, and as we approached the gate, I looked at him for guidance, and again he signaled to keep walking. The gate opened, I walked through and didn't see anyone but saw a path leading to a large building surrounded by a tall iron fence. At that moment, I had a strange feeling and turned back to look for him. My Guru was nowhere to be seen and I was a little bit afraid, and couldn't think properly. Even though, I struggled to keep my composure,

I continued walking towards the entrance, with the hope of finding him.

Just as I was about to ring the door bell, I was startled when the door suddenly opened as if someone was expecting me. Without any hesitation, I entered, expecting to see my Guru but for the very first time, I found myself face-to-face with Lord Rama. He greeted me with a big welcoming smile, and out of respect, I bowed and touched his feet. Then, I looked at him with the expectation that he would tell me something about my Guru but he was quiet and that was when I noticed that his skin was smooth and glowing. I knew of Lord Rama's divine greatness since my childhood by listening to stories from the Ramayana but although I was standing in his presence, my mind wondered restlessly about my Guru.

The door closed, and as I followed him, I saw groups of men in white clothing sitting around tables, eating. Then a woman appeared and invited us to have lunch. Lord Rama accepted, and we followed her into a room. On a table were a variety of dishes already prepared and laid out for us. The food tasted delicious, and we ate to our hearts content. Out of curiosity, my eyes roamed around the room noticing the tall windows with gold bars on the outside and the dishes were blue with gold patterns around the edges. Everything was sparkling clean. Even though I was worried about my Guru, strangely, I felt comfortable with Lord Rama.

At this time, I thought that my Guru and Lord Rama were two different saintly beings. In my quest to find answers, I was able to unearth through meditation that my Guru manifested himself as Lord Rama. In the guise of Lord Rama, I learned how to perfect my action and my mind towards righteousness. In doing so, I saw the truth about humanity and myself which helped me to become fearless, more confident and self-reliant. My Guru selflessly took responsibility, for removing my ignorance and mercifully revealed the way to higher thinking. Under his shelter, I had nothing to fear.

It was June 2010, and the weather was beautiful. I spent my lunch hours on Broadway and Wall Street, looking at the tourists while listening to their chatter. I heard them speaking in a diversity of languages, which I thought was intriguing and interesting. During one of my lunch-hour breaks, I went outdoors and was standing in front of a bank. The sun was overhead, and I remember stretching my neck as I looked at the sun, and pointing toward a building on Wall Street. I walked further up the street and stood in front of another bank. As I was standing there, facing the bank, I saw a flash of light coming towards me from the corner of my eye. I experienced a strange sensation, as if a bolt of lightning struck my lower back and then felt an intense rush of energy going up my spine. It was swift and painless. My body shook, and I staggered but didn't fall. I saw some people looking at me, and I calmly walked away. I didn't pay much attention to this incident and it was soon forgotten.

I returned to my classroom ready to work but thoughts of God took over my mind and I felt an irresistible urge to preach about him to my co-workers. My mind so absorbed in feelings of love and connection, that I enthusiastically wanted to share this. From their expression, I could see that they were surprised at my behavior and I decided not to preach to anyone else. Instantly my perception of God shifted to the forefront of my existence.

God's influence in my life was so strong that I didn't want to do anything wrong.

Then a few curious situations began to unfold that remained in my mind. Even though they seemed like normal everyday occurrences, they caught my attention and made me question myself. These incidents, became more frequent as the weeks went by. One day, during my lunch hour break, I went outdoors to get some fresh air and upon returning, someone said to me that there was a tremor on the top floors of the building where I worked. A couple of weeks later, I attended a workshop and while answering a question my voice sounded like someone else's. I didn't have a cold or any problem with my throat.

Soon after, someone from my knitting club asked me to bring a piece of material which represented my country of origin. I was taken back because I couldn't remember my birth country's name. Here again, I questioned myself. What was wrong with me but travelling in the train on my way home, jolted my memory and I remembered the name of my country. There was nothing wrong with me. In these instances, I believed that my Guru's infinite energy was present. I noticed that whenever anything unusual happened, something good would emerge in the end and enhanced my confidence. One day, I was asked to write a few words in a card because someone was leaving. I wanted to write something special because he was very generous with us over the years. I wrote, thanking him for his generosity and that he taught me a valuable lesson about giving. My co-workers read the card and were praising me for my choice of words. Their reaction was surprising and gave me the inspiration to continue writing.

As Lord Rama, my Guru's energy was like my shadow. Everywhere I went, I could feel his presence which had a huge impact on me. This energy was magnetic and I became a keen observer of nature. I was attracted to so many things, which made me feel like my eyes were opened to a brand world. What I had experienced only in visions materialized before my eyes. In my presence, these occurrences would be seen outdoors during the day. At night, I wrote whatever I saw, felt, or heard. After a couple weeks, of witnessing what I thought was impossible before, I knew, whatever I was seeing, and hearing wasn't my imagination, it was really happening. I saw him as my guardian angel, and a solid boulder that I could lean on in times of need. As Lord Rama, my Guru used normal everyday things that I've seen in the past to capture my attention. What I saw was unbelievable, and witnessing his divine energy gave me the impression that there was more to see. With this thought in my mind. I waited anxiously to witness what would happen next.

Every day, when the weather was favorable, my co-workers and I, would take the children for outdoor walks or to play at the park. On one such day, we took them to the park and on our way back, we saw a woman walking with her dog. As we approached them, the dog stopped suddenly, rolled on his back with his legs up, and made funny sounds. Then he turned on his stomach, with his legs outstretched in front of him and laid his head between his legs. He closed his eyes and we thought that he was resting but then got up within a second or two, wagging his tail. We stood there looking at him because the whole scenario was funny and rarely seen by us. All of us started laughing, and the woman began laughing too. She seemed a little bit embarrassed and asked the dog, *what are you doing*? That day, the dog entertained us.

Then on a hot summer day, we took the children to play with the sprinklers in Battery Park. The kids were excited and looking forward to play with the water and get wet. When we arrived there, one of the workers told us that the sprinkler was broken. The children were disappointed and as we were about to leave, I heard a noise like an engine starting up. Suddenly water was flowing and gushing everywhere and we were all in shock. The children eagerly began getting wet and filling their buckets. It seemed, my Guru couldn't resist granting the wishes of these innocent, pure hearts.

On a warm and beautiful spring day, we took the children for a stroll at the park. There was music and break-dancing which attracted a small group of people. We stopped by the dancers after seeing the smiles on the children's faces and thought that some of them would want to dance but they didn't. They stood quietly watching and I encouraged them to dance. Those who danced, continued until it was time for to us to leave the park. They had so much fun. At home that night, I was thinking about the children and their dancing and felt like Lord Rama was showing me, that as a teacher, it was my responsibility to get the children motivated and engaged in fun loving activities.

The next day, we went to Rockefeller Park and planned to stop by the duck pond because the children enjoyed looking at the fishes swimming in the pond. This was one of the places we often visited. The children usually sit or stand while looking at the fishes but this day as we were approaching the pond, the ducks started flying back and forth flapping their wings and quacking as if they were dancing to a secret melody. Then some birds joined in chirping and flying around the pond. It was a like a scene from a Broadway show and we all sat in surprise enjoying it. I think Lord Rama's jubilant energy, created this enjoyable environment just for the children. I was moved by this incredible performance and in my heart silently thanked him.

The following week as we were passing by the duck pond, a voice said, *look behind you*. I turned around and saw the most beautiful looking child following us. There was a radiance around him and to me he looked like an angelic apparition. His hair was white as snow and he wore a white tee shirt and diapers. He looked like he was three years old. For days, this vision stayed on my mind and refused to leave until I arrived at the understanding, that Lord Rama was showing me that he had accompanied us to the duck pond the week before. The ducks and the birds were celebrating his presence.

I went to a family function, and my sister and I decided to dance. While I was dancing, I felt like my hips and limbs were moving skillfully like an experienced dancer and I had no control over their movements. Afterwards, quite a few people complimented us, and someone said on the microphone that this was the first time he had witnessed dancing of this kind. I was never a good dancer and was in shock with my performance. I completely avoided dancing before because I always felt like I had two left feet. My husband was a good dancer and so were my daughters. I've always wanted to learn how to dance and it was always at the back of my mind that if I know how to dance, then

I can certainly join them on the dance floor. This was one of many instances where Lord Rama's energy gave me confidence and courage to go beyond my limitations.

A week or two later, I was dancing with three-year-old children in the classroom, and I noticed one of the children was happily dancing, perfectly in tune with the music. After seeing her dance a few more times, I told one of my co-workers that I had recently danced at my family's function and that was how I danced. It occurred to me that Lord Rama placed me among these pure hearts and orchestrated profound lessons to help me grow. His messages were often simple but contained a deeper meaning. I realized that he was always encouraging me to do all the things, I wouldn't do in the past and he was also showing me that I am capable of doing them with finesse. He was like a doctor injecting courage and confidence in me. My feelings for Lord Rama were indescribable and I was overwhelmed by this show of care and love for me. His kindness struck me like lightning and left me paralyzed with gratitude. I felt tall, knowing that he was promoting me to greater knowledge.

In meditation, I focused all my attention on Lord Rama and what he was teaching me. As his student, I was working hard and always wanted to know what I would see or feel next. At night, I wrote whatever I saw or witnessed during the day. I knew that these experiences were unique and important. I willing prepared myself to work diligently to please him, knowing that this opportunity would never repeat itself again, not in my lifetime. I was more than grateful and thought of him constantly.

CHAPTER ELEVEN

Lord Rama's Lessons

HIS LESSONS CAME TO ME in unusual ways and I did not understand them until much later. He took hold of my life and everything in it. He crafted simple unimaginable experiences to rectify the shortcomings in my life at home and at work. I marveled whenever he displayed his original ideas. Then he would orchestrate situations and events to illuminate my inner world.

It was a mild spring day that my co-workers and I decided to spend sometime in the park during our lunch hour enjoying the beautiful weather. I saw bunches of pink roses and couldn't resist taking a closer look. I left them to go and had to climb on a concrete wall enclosing a green space. There was a photographer taking pictures of a female model posing by the Hudson River, and other people were sitting leisurely, enjoying the weather. After admiring the roses, I decided to walk back to rejoin my friends, but when I tried walking my feet moved in a zigzag motion, even though I tried to walk properly, I couldn't control my feet or balance my legs. After struggling for about two minutes, I was able to walk like my usual self again. I was so embarrassed, not realizing at the time that he was teaching me something very important. He wanted me to find a balance in my worldly life, as my awareness expanded and I elevated spiritually.

One Monday morning, we took the children to the park and gave them balls to play with. We played soccer and when I kicked the ball it rolled in a straight line for a long, distance. It wasn't a kick with force and I was as surprised as everyone else. I wasn't a young person, I was already in my sixties and I was shocked at myself. I never had any interest in playing soccer before and never kicked a ball this far. This was all new to me. Here again another lesson learned. Age is just a number. Everyone has the ability to achieve success. Just do whatever you want to do and forget, how old you are.

One day, I was walking home in the rain without an umbrella because, I felt it was too heavy to carry. When I reached home, my clothes were surprisingly dry, with just a few raindrops here and there. There were other times like this, when I was convinced that Lord Rama was showing me his ability *to control the elements*. When I was outdoors during the hot summer days and thinking how hot and uncomfortable it was, instantaneously a gust of cool refreshing breeze would appear out of nowhere. To make me feel his presence, the sun's reflection against the glass windows on the buildings, lit the pavement as I walked. If I was going out in the night, the moon's protective gaze seemed to follow our car to and from its destination. I saw Lord Rama in the sun and the moon. I thought he was watching and protecting my every move. I felt like the sun and the moon were my security guards. Whenever I was out doors, during the day, I searched for the sun and when I was going out in the night, I searched for the moon. Once I saw them, I felt secure.

I focused on Lord Rama and lost interest in everyone and everything. I didn't watch television, and refrain from gossiping with my sisters. Whenever I did a lot of work around the house, I found quarters mostly on the rugs next to my feet. This had never happened before, and when I was thinking, *why is this happening*? Words rushed into my mind, *whoever works for me gets paid.* Here Lord Rama was telling me, the more I immersed myself in devotion and meditation, I will earn his treasure which is eternal. I understood that he wasn't going to spoil me, and if I wanted to achieve anything in my life time, I had to make sacrifices and work hard.

When Lord Rama was teaching me his countenance was serious yet he appeared to be gentle, approachable and calm. There were moments when he allowed me to see that he was observing my actions. This gave me confidence and the zest to work harder to fulfill his expectations. His blessings gave me vitality and sharpened the blades in my mind. My Guru as Lord Rama was phenomenal. His strategy was brilliant and he was meticulous. Everything he touched in my life turned into a gold bullion. It was, like he added his special brand of ingredients to flavor my life which exploded with desires to reach for the stars. I never envisioned, that this iconic figure would selflessly take the initiative to lead me on this path of righteous and truth. My appreciation for my Guru reached the stars.

CHAPTER TWELVE

Humanitarian Lessons

LORD RAMA ALSO USED WORDS and visions to teach me. These visions contained lessons about humanity. In meditation, he allowed me to accompany him to different places as he observed people of all nationality and classes. As his teachings intensified, my thirst for learning grew and I craved for more.

Vision: One

In this vision, we walked in a forest surrounded by trees of all description. Sturdy, old, young, tall, short, and leafy ones. Lord Rama was looking keenly, at each one of them. Then he took me on top of a mountain and again he was looking at everything around us. When I glanced at him, he appeared concerned. I believed, Lord Rama was using the trees to show me that despite hazardous climate conditions, the trees stood tall and were striving.

The mountain represented strength. He knew that I needed to learn how to grow in any conditions, to become stronger.

Vision: Two

Lord Rama held my hand, and as we floated up towards the sky, I noticed that he was looking down. I followed his gaze curious to know what he was looking at. There were people working in the fields and when I glanced at him, I saw his expression soften. There was compassion in his eyes, not because they were working but because they looked tired and worn out. Within seconds, these words rushed into my mind: *My people, my people.*

Vision: Three

We were standing in a class room with some children and their teachers. I was standing quietly, next to him with folded arms listening, and observing as well. He took his time, looking here, there and everywhere. Lord Rama was doing his own evaluation.

Vision: Four

One night, I was meditating and saw Lord Rama having a conversation with me and the words that surfaced in my mind were: I came, I saw and I've chosen. I believed Lord Rama planted the seeds of rejuvenation within me. At that time, I felt so connected and grateful to receive his messages which I considered to be everlasting and sacred.

Lord Rama didn't waste any time. He showed me that I had to devote myself if I wanted to acquire knowledge of any kind. My first lesson was about observation. As my divine mentor, he never smiled while he was teaching me and looked stern. His stern expression spoke to me and I knew that I have to pay attention, concentrate, and learn. I also wanted to prove that I was capable and could do it. Frequently in meditation, I saw us at the library, with him opening several books and I standing quietly beside him, trying to understand and retain everything he was teaching me. Just the thought of him taking his time to bless me with the highest knowledge, drowned me in gratitude. I wanted to ask him, *who am I Lord Rama and why am I being treated like royalty*? Later, when I had the urge to write what I saw in visions, the words came naturally. I read and learned from the written materials. Another one of his brilliant teaching ideas that only a saintly being or God can make happen to a human being.

Many times, I found myself looking at people and studying them. During this time, I was fascinated with people and admired them. To me, their faces were mirrors telling me their stories. When I saw happy and healthy people, I was delighted, when I saw sad and struggling ones, I was worried and when I saw the sick and poor, I was hurting. One day, I was in the train and someone was standing in front of me. He was facing me with his head bent. He seemed disturbed and uncared for. I couldn't take my eyes off him and unexpectedly my silent thoughts were interrupted. In my mind, I heard him praying and asking God not to forget him and even though he wasn't saying anything, I felt his pain. I wanted to tell him that God loves him and would never leave him and one day God would fulfill his wishes. I felt sympathy for him and hoped that something positive would happen soon to change his life for the better. Seeing this person made me feel like I don't deserve this miracle in my life, and that this person needed it more than I do.

After studying and observing a lot of people, I arrived at the conclusion that so many are willing to serve God and change for the better. I know that people are God's wealth and treasures and all he wants, is for us to build our castles in both worlds, devote some of our time to him. We all have this shining light within us, let us use it and benefit from this luminous light. Constantly, he reveals his divine messages to us, understanding them is time consuming but rewarding. I learned after these lessons with Lord Rama that kindness, patience, tolerance, truth, and understanding can work miracles with people.

My second lesson with Lord Rama was about honesty and trust. He was quick in displaying an example of how, what and when to speak. He was also teaching me to speak the truth without hurting anyone and by doing this, I would gain the trust of others. An opportunity presented itself when I was retiring from my job and the school was sending me off with a luncheon party. I knew I had to give a speech and planned to say a few words from a thank you letter, I had written. Yet when I opened my mouth divine wisdom took over. Words flowed easily without any effort from me. I continued to say things that were not premediated. Before I would worry for days and be nervous but this time it was different. I was brave and spoke with confidence and flare. I was proud of myself and rejoiced in God's blessings.

All my life, I was a quiet and an easy going person. I strive and blossom in calm, peaceful environments, and to be this fearless was an eye opener for me. I welcomed this new skill and since then, can deliver a good speech without having to prepare too much. Whatever was lacking or needs improvement in my life, Lord Rama used every opportunity, to show me how it was done. Memories like this one put a stamp in my heart and will remain there until the end of time. I've never experienced anything like this before and my devotion for him increased immensely. Nothing can compare to my Guru's energy. For me it was like turning over a new leaf, and finding myself in a different category. Because of him, I was adding skills after skills to my professional life's resume.

My third lesson was about people and how to work with different personalities and manage conflicts. This was difficult but intriguing for me. When problems surfaced in my everyday life, Lord Rama allowed me to travel through the situations and guided me in meditation to find a fair solution. I witnessed how my co-workers reacted in stressful and non-stressful situations. As a teacher of toddlers, the most stressful situations in the classroom were when biting occurs, constant crying, and when children were hurt. Incidents like these caused anxiety among us. As teachers, our job was to keep the children safe and when an accident occurred, we felt like we've failed. Then we have to explain to the parents and administration how, when and why it happened. When I was faced with similar situations, how to address them, came naturally, which I couldn't do before. I knew that Lord Rama was teaching me how to solve my everyday life challenges and also how to engage with others in a positive way. I learned, that when you do things differently in a smart and decent way, others will respect you. This ideology made my working life enjoyable, instead of being stressful and at home little things didn't bother me anymore. I was empowered by his love and compassion but more so by whatever he was teaching me.

My mind was over flowing with pure thoughts of Lord Rama and God. I was in a different world where nothing else matters, when all of a sudden the words, *Wall Street,* disrupted my quiet thoughts, feelings of contentment, and the words lingered. A couple of days later, unexpectedly the words, *Wall Street be prepared, I am coming,* rushed in my mind again followed by the words *invest in metals.* These words entered my mind, like heavy raindrops splashing against the window panes. I personally, knew nothing about stocks, trading and investing. I was never interested in the stock exchange or Wall Street but suddenly, I found myself drawn to Wall Street. During my lunch hours, I walked around, admired the buildings that lined the streets, the flowering plants, and looked at the masses of tourists moving at a leisurely pace enjoying the beautiful, crisp spring weather. Wall Street was on my mind all the time and wouldn't leave me alone. I had a premonition that something of importance would occur there.

CHAPTER THIRTEEN

God Intervened

DAYS LATER, I WOKE UP with Lord Rama on my mind, not knowing that I would witness the grandest sight on earth. God gave me the ultimate experience that day. As usual, I went to Wall Street during my lunch hour and stood looking at the stock market index billboard. I don't know why I was drawn to the numbers on that board. Then I stood there lazily enjoying the weather when something caught my eyes. A magnificent sight, moving slowly towards me that I will never forget. I was breathless, numb and couldn't move. To my amazement, I saw not only Lord Rama but Lord Krishna, Lord Shiva, and Lord Hanuman walking toward me. What a place to see them, Wall Street. I felt like I stepped into the unknown, God's country and that day, I saw God in everyone there.

The atmosphere seemed different suddenly and I couldn't believe my eyes. Here I was in the company of the highest of highest. They were gorgeous and magnificent looking.

Their features were flawless and beyond beautiful. Their smiles took my breath away and I questioned myself, *am I dreaming?* I wasn't. The aura around them was electrifying. I bowed and touched their feet one after the other. They touched my head, giving me their blessings in return. I felt honored to be in their company. Just looking at them gave me the strength to ignore everyone and to do whatever God wanted.

Wall Street was packed with people, and receiving God's blessings in the presence of all these people was amazing. Wow! I'd never dreamed or imagined that God would elevate my confidence this way. Am I grateful? Of course and I cannot describe the enormity of my feelings for him. I realized that God's grace was showered upon me and brought divinity into my life. That day, I experienced the most precious gift from God, being able to see Lord Rama, Lord Hanuman, Lord Krishna and Lord Shiva. They seemed happy, and so was I. I saw in them strength, confidence, wisdom, greatness, and pride. I felt love for them in the purest form and instantly realized how lucky I was to be among the greatest of greatest. I closed my eyes for a minute thanking God and when I opened them, they were gone. Anyway, my lunch hour was over and I returned to my classroom ready to work. After this miracle, I felt so much affection for people because on that special day, when I looked at them, I felt connected to all of humanity.

As the months went by and I began recollecting this incident. I knew that this was a rare experience and asked myself again and again, how can I not love God more than myself? How can I repay him? *Only with devotion.* Such a small sacrifice from me compared to the humungous opportunity he gave me. I realized that this was what my Guru was telling me in the beginning, when I saw myself crossing over that bridge and seeing the deities as little children celebrating. It meant, that God would give me access to meet, greet and mingle with the widely worshipped Hindu deities, Lord Rama, Lord Hanuman, the ardent devotee of Lord Rama, Lord Krishna, the beloved eighth avatar of the Hindu God Vishnu and Lord Shiva, the destroyer and restorer in the sacred Hindu Trinity. Where else but on the grounds of Wall Street. My Guru's presence and meditation opened the gates to my inner world where God resides.

Any doubts about Lord Rama's presence in my life disappeared and I felt safe and protected. On several occasions when I walked, it felt like my body was stretched and I was walking tall, observing, listening, and watching everyone. I was like a detective gathering information and at the same time learning about the people and everything else. I couldn't stay indoors, I had to be out and about during my lunch breaks and once outdoors, I would take long walks along the Hudson River and admired all the beauty and greenery surrounding me. The water, the boats, the flowers, the trees and the breathtaking view of the New Jersey Shore. As the days went by, I noticed a difference in me. Whenever, I was in the company of others, I remained quiet, listened to everyone and didn't join in any conversation. I was in a world of my own with God and Lord Ram always in my thoughts. I wanted to close my eyes, meditate, see Lord Rama and be in solitude with God as much as possible. Their presence made me feel like I was so smart and I gained an intense appreciation for all God's creations.

I felt deeply connected to the sun, the moon, and the wind. As I mentioned earlier, I thought they were my security guards. When I was in doubt about the sun following me, the doubts were quickly erased as I felt the scorching heat of the sun on my back. On weekends, if I was lazy and wanted to sleep longer, the sun's reflection found a way to wake me up. To me the sun was my constant companion, following me everywhere. Sometimes, when I was feeling alone on a rainy day, I looked at the sky and saw the moon appearing and then disappearing behind the clouds, as if saying to me, *I am here*. I felt better. If I saw the sun in the mornings on my way to work, I instantly assumed the day would be a good one. My assumption was usually correct. I considered the moon, sun, and the wind to be my best friends. I knew that they were connected to Lord Rama and this was his doing. He gave me the best of the best treatment. There was no need to ask for anything.

On hot summer days, the wind came to my rescue and the moon was my escort during the nights. These were my thoughts then. I thanked Lord Rama many times a day for his compassion. Several times, when I was sleeping, the reflection of the moon on my bed woke me up. I would get out of bed, move the curtains, looked at the moon, and then go back to bed. When I was alone, I reflected on the moon, sun, and the wind. I often wondered, *why is this happening? I've never had experiences like these before.* I considered Lord Rama to be the generator that brings light into our lives and the pipe line that supply us with water to keep us running. With him beside me, everything is possible and attainable. When I was a child, I heard the priests preaching in their sermons over and over again that God controls everything.

After having these experiences, I now know, that God is the supreme power house of the universe.

The Divine continued to show me how incredible God can be in one's life, if he is known. I was reminded of this, when I was entering the airport on my trip to Rome to join my husband's twin sisters, in celebrating their eightieth birthday. There was this sudden gust of wind which had my hair flying in all directions. We laughed at my disheveled appearance but for me, it meant that God was with us. Then on our flight to Rome, we encountered some turbulence which shook the plane a little. I was scared, closed my eyes and began meditating, when I had a vision of Lord Rama with his arms outstretched under the plane. My fear disintegrated immediately. With a clean slate on my mind and knowing that he was on board, I knew that nothing would go wrong and fell into a deep sleep.

During our stay in Rome, we visited the Vatican City and everywhere I looked, I saw God's handiwork. I began to imagine what it would be like, living in this kind of environment. How would I feel, surrounded by a rainbow of colors? Would I feel his presence and dream of saintly beings hovering over me? Or see angels in a circle fluttering their wings? One thing, I know for sure, the paintings and sculptures awakened a burst of creative ideas within me and I felt the spiritual purpose of my visit here was to gain more inspiration.

It was time to return home and that morning the weather was foggy. On our way to the airport, the cab driver told us that sometimes, the flights were cancelled because of the fog. When I heard this, I was concerned about the long hours, we would have to wait at the airport if our flight was cancelled. Here again, I experienced my Guru's compassion, while we were sitting in the airport waiting to join the plane. I was reading a magazine and from the corner of my eye, saw a young pigeon with glistening feathers walking around the area, where I was sitting with some people. Looking at it, made me feel like this pigeon was well taken care of. It lingered for a while, walking and watching everyone and then it was gone. I believed, this was a sign from my Guru, telling me that he was with us. Why worry, when I have the Supreme with me? The fog cleared and the flight took off, on time.

CHAPTER FOURTEEN

God's Revelation

MY EDUCATION WITH LORD RAMA moved at a fast pace, and I was so grateful for our sacred bond. I considered him to be my security blanket as well as my protector. He was everything I imagined him to be and more. Listening to devotional songs about him constantly, made me feel closer to him and I was at peace with myself. Lord Rama knew how my mind works and what needed to be improved. He made me aware of my short comings and showed me how to overcome them. I was too quiet. I needed to be bolder, braver and be able to defend myself in any given situation. He knew, that others could take advantage of my naïve nature.

Sooner than I thought, a conflicting situation came into existence that I was very uncomfortable with. When I was faced with this kind of dilemma in the past, I didn't know, how to assertively defend myself. This time, I was presented with an opportunity to grow and use all that I was taught, to get through it. I, on the other hand, wanted to prove to myself that I've learned and most importantly, I didn't want to disappoint my Guru. With a little planning, and remembering what he taught me, I approached this situation like a professional. How by using a calm, controlled, and friendly voice in dialogue. Where, in a relaxed and private atmosphere. When, at the right time. It worked like an ace and I was deliriously happy knowing that I didn't disappoint my Guru or myself.

After this, I encountered a couple more challenges which made me very unhappy and I was seriously thinking of quitting my job. The path to divine wisdom is not easy, especially when I didn't understand my Guru's good intentions. Hidden in all these challenges were valuable lessons to learn. My Guru wasn't creating these rough patches to upset me, he was simply exposing me to different situations and showing me how to resolve them peacefully. The rough patches were like workshops, where I was supposed to learn something new each time. In my ignorance, I didn't understand what he was doing and was still toying with the idea of quitting my job. My Guru came to my rescue with a miraculous solution which prevented me from making a wrong decision.

One day, my co-workers went to lunch while the children were taking their afternoon nap. I was sitting alone in the dimly lit, quiet class room thinking about which activities, I should prepare for the afternoon session when I experienced something magical. For me, it seemed like my Guru waved his magic wand, enclosing my body with a thin veil, and a pure sensation engulfed my entire being. I felt pure. The hairs on my arms stood up, my body was still and I couldn't move for a few minutes. Then slowly, I felt like the veil was uplifted and that pure feeling slowly vanished. Amazed and trembling, I got up and stood where I was for a couple of minutes to catch my breath, and couldn't believe the magnitude of what I felt. I believed that this was his way of embracing me and saying, *keep your job.* He knew how I was feeling and once again responded to my worries. I wanted to jump and scream for joy. Immediately, all the negativity in my mind cleared. This feeling of purity and love made me feel like I was a new person. I didn't quit my job and never regretted my decision. My attitude towards making hasty decisions changed. Now, I take my time, think and when I am absolutely sure, only then, will I make a commitment. In the future, if I do make a mistake, I will consider it to be a new lesson learned.

That afternoon when I was leaving my work place, my body was filled with new vigor and vitality. I held my head high and walked briskly to the subway. I was determined to overcome all my fears and difficulties in the future. Inwardly, I rejoiced at my Guru's revelation which changed me from a meek mouse into a roaring lion and after this incident, I found my voice and was able to use it. Since I couldn't share my feelings with anyone, this secret remained with my Guru and me.

I realized now that all the unusual occurrences were intended not to hurt me but to teach me life lessons. Lord Rama orchestrated and implemented real situations in my working life and allowed me to see other people's reactions and hear their opinions. Sometimes, he would show me scenarios of myself working with my co-workers, as if I was watching a series on television. I learned and benefited immensely from his lessons of greater knowledge. As the days went by, I decided to forge ahead, aiming only towards happiness and peace of mind. My life had a new meaning, a new purpose and a new direction.

CHAPTER FIFTEEN

God's Miracles

THIS WAS WHEN HE GAVE me another unforgettable experience. Early one morning, I was travelling in the train to work. I closed my eyes and was thinking about Lord Rama and God, when I heard voices, praying and asking God to help them. Some were complaining and others were thanking and praising him. I saw faces and heard their stories. When I opened my eyes and looked at people in the train, I could hear their thoughts. I felt their pain and joy. This happened frequently for about a week and then stopped. That day on my way home, some words entered my mind and they were: *I succumbed to his good intentions and was able to see the world through his eyes.* In surrendering to God's will, I gained God's wisdom and attributes. God sees and knows everything about each one of us. Just imagine how he feels when we are walking on the wrong path. I often wondered, how he is able to deal with all of us.

During my commute to work, I looked at so many faces in the train. I didn't think about color, class or religion, what I saw were human beings willing to help another human being. So many, willingly gave me their seats, especially when the train was packed or in the afternoon when I was tired and heading home. Their kind acts made a difference in my daily life. One day, I was meditating in the train and someone came and sat across from me, I opened my eyes for a second and felt positive energy from his direction. His eyes were closed as if he was also meditating and at that moment, I felt we all have this untapped ability to find inner peace and could share it with others.

Another time, I was writing in the train. My hand moved over the page with speed and a purpose of its own and this is what was written.

To all beings, I am yours, and you are mine,
I love you and you love me,
Make me proud.
To my daughters, the lights of my life: I love you both.
To my husband: I love you. Thank you for your patience.
To my grandsons: I love you, guys.
To my sisters, nieces, nephews, and relatives, I love you all.

To me, when I read it, the wording gave me the impression that this was a farewell gesture from Lord Rama. My Guru's work as Lord Rama was ending and I won't see him as Lord Rama in meditation again. I would never forget, how he walked with me, to show me the truth about myself and others. My Guru sees goodness in all his disciples and because of him, I saw goodness in everyone. We need to apply goodness in our lives and experience the bliss. As for me, a new person evolved from my inner world.

When I walked from the train station to work that morning, I looked up at the sky and saw the clouds moving. I had the feeling, that the clouds were also sending me the same message. In the train on my way home, I felt devastated. I wanted to go with him, and when this thought was swirling in my head, words came quickly and they were: *You have a family. They need you, and you need them.* When his energy was circulating around me, I felt safe and secured knowing that he was in my life guiding me through the bad and good times. I've always admired the uniqueness of his lessons and how he designed and presented them. I was inspired and yearned for more. The thought of not seeing him, traumatized me. When I was thinking how to go on without him, these words, *heal thy self* immediately sprinted into my mind.

Lord Rama, didn't say that he was leaving and even though, I continued to meditate, I didn't see him again in meditation. I missed seeing him but he had given me the wisdom and confidence to be on my own. I knew that if I ever needed him, he would be there. My lunch hours were spent in the school building in solitude, reading or learning new words from a pocket dictionary. I wasn't ready to socialize and didn't pay attention to anyone. I needed, to be alone and process my experiences. I also focused on my work and was even more sensitive to the children's wellbeing and their needs. In class, new ideas came instantly and I was able to set up activities of interest for the children which they enjoyed immensely. Somehow, I knew what to do to hold their attention for longer periods of time than before, and this proved to be fruitful. I was satisfied with my work ethic.

At home my conversations with my sisters were different. Instead of engaging in gossip, we talked about our parents, our child hood memories and our children. I allowed them to do most of the talking and I listened. If I see people begging or homeless, my heart would hurt and wished that I could help them. I also noticed some changes in my behavior. At lunch time our team of teachers would have discussions on matters pertaining to our classroom and the children. Normally I would sit and listen but I found myself joining in with smart suggestions. In the class room, my actions were commendable by my colleagues. I knew what to do, when and how to inspire the children and hold their attention. Afterwards, I would reflect on my actions and knew that my Guru was helping me. I could never forget how he painstakingly showed me step by step to solve problems. He taught me to listen, use dialogue with a soft tone, be kind, and understanding in challenging situations.

I was tempted numerous times, to tell everyone about him but I couldn't bring myself to say the words. When I tried, I felt like something was holding me back. I knew that the timing wasn't right and had to delete that thought completely from my mind but this is what I would have told them. *Victory to my Guru, a one-of-a kind and resourceful one. He feels compassion for everyone. Come! Come! He is here for all of us to take advantage of. Join freely in the peace and happiness. He brings light into our lives, and when there is a need he gives us a gentle push.*

CHAPTER SIXTEEN

Knowledge Gained

WHILE I WAS GOING THROUGH difficult challenges,
Lord Rama graciously taught me:

To depend on myself,
Work for everything I want,
Choose my friends wisely,
To forgive and forget,
Be fearless and strong,
Pay whoever works for me,
Proceed with positive thoughts,
Have compassion for everyone,
Be humble,
Be myself and be realistic,
Have affection for all people,
Respect others, even when I am upset,
Work diligently and have no fear,
Admire and give credit to those who deserves it,

VR

Value my achievements,
Pay attention to cleanliness,
Be true to myself and others,
Do not succumb to temptations,
That life is living for yourself but caring for others,
That everyone will achieve achievements due to his or her
own capabilities,
That great stories emerge from our everyday experiences,
That people are important and are God's most prized asset,
When God looks down on earth, all he sees are his children.

When my Guru came to me as Lord Rama in meditation, I was in dire need of guidance. His teachings helped me greatly when my job was hiring young college graduates as substitute teachers with the intention of making them permanent. I was in a competitive situation and being an older teacher had to prove my worth. I worked hard and gained the respect of my administrator. I showed everyone that I was capable of working under any circumstances. I had the experience and creative knowledge to make life in the classroom easy and inspiring. The ones who worked co-operatively and were willing to learn became permanent teachers at the end of the school year. Friendly project competitions among us were implemented in the classroom for the children and we considered them to be successful, only when the children participated and enjoyed themselves tremendously. There were days when we were surprised at the children's reaction as well. I realized then that I was making a difference and it was because of my Guru's influence. My life was like a tree, planted in fertile soil which grew tall with branches spreading out in all directions. The teachers recognized that I had acquired skills that they could benefit from. I shared willingly and had great satisfaction in doing so. I continued to work harmoniously with others and at the end of the school year, had reached retirement age and was asked to retire. This came as a surprise and even though I didn't plan on retiring so soon, I accepted their offer. As my retirement day was approaching, I felt nervous and realized that I made a big mistake. I wanted to continue working so badly that I prayed about it. My prayers were answered when I heard that they were hiring substitute teachers. I asked administration if I could remain and work as a substitute teacher. They agreed. I was happy because I could continue to do what I enjoyed the most, which was being in the classroom with the children.

As a substitute teacher, I was given the opportunity to work in a number of classrooms and after working for a few weeks, I saw my full potential and realized that I can work independently. With confidence, I began to work harder and on many occasions, I was sent to work with children who needed extra support. I knew how to calm and soothe them. This also came naturally. At the end of each day, I was rewarded with a sense of satisfaction and fulfillment. Surprisingly, the skills I displayed when my Guru's energy was around, remained with me and proved to be so beneficial. I considered them to be my prized possessions and applied them in my work every day.

I couldn't believe how extensive my growth was in all areas of my life. I knew, it was only because of my Guru blessings and the wisdom he imbedded in me through his teachings. I felt indebted and close to God and my Guru. I was at peace knowing that they were in my life and had faith that they would be my partners in all my future projects. I will always be grateful that my Guru selflessly played the roles of both my parents and God, by maneuvering my life in the direction, which he knew was best for me.

CHAPTER SEVENTEEN

My Guru's Re-appearance

ONE MORNING, I WAS MEDITATING and was thrilled with a few unexpected surprises. I saw myself fast asleep in a white hammock. Lord Shiva and Lord Krishna were pacing the floors waiting for me to wake up. When I woke up, they rushed towards me and quickly offered me a glass of milk and cookies. There were two small wooden tables placed against a whitewashed wall. One table had several dishes of sweets dripping with honey. Beautiful silks and jewelry were displayed elegantly on the other one. In my vision, I saw myself in a dilemma and couldn't decide which table I should go to first. Should I touch the beautiful silks with jewelry or rush towards the sweets dripping with honey. I went for the yummy delicacies. Then I saw myself running around and playing. Lord Krishna was burning incense and with one hand on my head, he placed a lamp in front of me, and my beloved Guru suddenly appeared surrounded by lighted lanterns. Seeing him made me feel like the sun had arrived. Instinctively, I ran and stood looking at him, it brought back memories of the past and words began running a marathon in my thoughts, the leisurely walks we had while enjoying nature, sitting on an elephant with him walking beside me, his teachings and everything I learned from him. My God came and I was deliriously happy to see him again. I felt like he went on a vacation and returned to continue his work with me.

A few days later, I had a vision that I never envisioned was possible. One Saturday morning, I was working on my computer and after a while my eyes felt tired. I decided to take a break. I closed my eyes with my head resting on the back of my chair and Lord Ganesh appeared in my vision. He was fast asleep and after a while, he opened his eyes and looked at me. I was surprised and my mind went blank. Then my mind instantly wandered in God's world. I couldn't believe what I was seeing but whole heartedly welcomed the magnificent sight of him. He looked serene and peaceful and his color was a unique, light shade of pink. For me, this was one of the most beautiful images that I have ever seen of him. This had a huge impact on me for a couple of days. I was astounded, happy and excited all at the same time. I went down on my knees and thanked him for his appearance in my vision and as usual asked myself why but prior to this vision, I remembered singing continuously one of his devotional songs in the past and my sudden interest in this song had baffled me. I questioned myself a hundred times, why. It didn't cross my mind then, that I was working towards a golden opportunity to have him clear the way for a smooth and safe journey. After all, he is known as the remover of obstacles in the Hindu tradition. In my heart, I knew that my Guru would ultimately help and protect me always, and in meditation, I would gain access to higher spiritual knowledge.

Then on a beautiful summer day, when I was taking a nap after working in my garden, I had a dream and saw the outline of a man with me in a room filled with books. He had shoulder length wavy, blond hair. He opened a book and was turning the pages and seemed like he was explaining something to me. I was standing next to him, listening and trying to grasp whatever he was teaching. I saw myself engrossed in his lessons and having conversations with him. Even though he had the same serious look like Lord Rama, there was also a gentle demeanor about him. I know what that look meant. Pay attention and learn. After I woke up, I was overwhelmed with the thought of this saintly apparition teaching me, then the following words interrupted my thoughts and they were: *You are God's creation and you are created like everyone else. You're entitled to all the privileges this world has to offer,* meaning that I will be given opportunities to rise above and beyond my limitations. One such occasion was when a cousin of mine died. He and my youngest sister were close buddies when he was alive. I went to the wake and as soon as I entered the funeral parlor, my sister quickly pulled me aside and asked if I could write a few words about the departed. She promised that she would accompany me to the podium. I agreed and wrote the speech in five minutes on tissue paper. After I read it, I couldn't believe how brave I was. I was impressed with myself and knew that this was only because of my Guru's boundless effort, in fostering my capabilities.

After this revelation, it was like starting to walk alone

on a newly paved road and not knowing which direction to take. My Guru didn't hesitate. His response was quick. Words rained down from above to rescue and helped me to clear all the uncertainty in my mind. They showed me how to go about living this new life and they were:

Comprehend and acknowledge your new status,
Connect the puzzle pieces together, the old and the new you,
Show others that you have changed,
Build trust in yourself and others,
Have confidence and serve whenever the occasion arises,
Display some of the gifts that you have earned,
Prove that I taught you well and you learned.

With these words my Guru laid out the path forward. He also gave the new me, the tools to navigate every area of my life. I felt, like I had gained enough knowledge and was well equipped to live a meaningful life.

In the early stages of my spiritual journey, my Guru took the responsibility of a parent and allowed me to see him constantly in visions, as my spiritual master. As I progressed and grew under his supervision, he decided that it was time to remove himself from my visions. Then he derived a new method to keep in touch with me and his means of communicating was by transmitting words into my thoughts, which add to my perception of myself and the world. On many occasions, when I encountered difficult people, I knew what to do and was able to defuse any situation. Whenever this happened, I would immediately give thanks to my Guru and wished that I could do something in return for him.

During the spring and summer months, I spent hours

outdoors, enjoying the beautiful weather, and admired the multi-colored butterflies among the flowering plants. I looked at the sky and watched the clouds moving, sometimes fast, sometimes slow or not at all. The white clouds looked like giant cotton balls, stretched out in a variety of shapes and sizes. I listened to the birds in the trees, singing their melodious lullabies, while jumping from branch to branch. These simple acts from nature, inspired creativity in my mind and with my daughter, spent many hours planting and re-planting flowers in my little garden. Every year, there was always a rose, a flower or a plant that found a place in our hearts and together, we learned something new. The joy of nature is contagious especially when the garden is in full bloom. We received many compliments from people passing by and made new friends with strangers who shared our interest in gardening. There was a difference in my life, it was settled, and peaceful.

Every morning, on my way to the subway, I had to cross a busy street near a school and always noticed the crossing guard helping the children. This morning, because I was going to work later than I had the previous mornings, I wondered if she would be there. She wasn't. While this thought was still on my mind, there was a sudden gust of wind, which blew a one-gallon plastic bottle onto the center of the road. After I crossed the road, a car came and ran over the bottle. The sound was deafening and the car stopped. I turned around with the thought that something was wrong but fortunately nothing happened. As I continued walking to the subway, an idea asserted itself in my mind and a story named "The Crossing Guard" was written. Writing this story so quickly, brought back memories of the other stories I had written, when my Guru's enormous energy was circulating around me. Here I discovered, that once I stay connected through meditation, my creativity skills would not diminish, but will continue to flourish.

CHAPTER EIGHTEEN

Understanding His Mission

THROUGH MEDITATION, THE ESSENCE OF my Guru's teachings came to light. That one can connect with God and know the truth about oneself. This realization took my breath away and I was intoxicated with appreciation and affection for this Honorable Divine Being. Words cannot describe the volume of my feelings for him. I feel indebted, grateful and honored to have him in my life and I am more than willing to live my life according to his teachings. A Guru acts as the bridge between his disciples and God, and with his grace, guides them towards self - realization.

He gifted me instantaneous clarity that had eluded me for so long and I experienced an explosion of true understanding. My sacred journey was all about knowing how to connect with God, know the truth about my Guru, humanity, myself and discovering my capabilities. I revel at this understanding and I can now savor the delicacies of his blessings. Now I understand, why I had the compelling urge and obsessive determination to write this story. My Guru wanted me to sincerely devote myself to meditation, because through this course of action, the highest truth would be revealed. My Guru is above and beyond any limitations.

My goal was to do everything the right way and implement the knowledge that I've gained so far into my life. I tried not to make the same mistakes. I wanted to show my Guru that I have changed and that I've learned. Then a question entered in my thoughts and it was, *which religion should I embrace?* The answer I received was, *you have no religion because I have no religion.* I believe that these words meant that, *as his disciple, my religious background was not important.* My Guru is a noble soul who accepts all beings under his shelter.

Early one rainy morning, I was waiting for the train at the Brighton Beach Subway Station, and I was thinking about Lord Ganesh. I entered the train, and as usual sat by the window. On the floor next to my feet was a long white feather that immediately caught my eyes. It was striking to me that it remained unsoiled and looked untouched. After staring at it for a while, I began to think that the feather was a sign of a guardian angel escorting me to work. With this thought in my mind, I was eager to reach my work place and start working, with an expectation that something exceptional would occur. That day, the atmosphere was different in the class-room and it affected the children and the teachers positively. The children happily engaged themselves in the daily activities and there was calm in our working environment throughout the day. At the end of the day, everyone was peaceful and stress free. I silently thanked my guardian angel and when I woke up the next morning, these words were on my mind. *Every day is a new beginning, with a new ending, and yesterday, yes, yesterday, is in the past.* Here my Guru was telling me to forget the past and look forward to living a new and exemplary life.

For me, this new way of living my life meant that God comes first before everything else. During one of our annual vacation, this concept was implemented in our vacation itinerary, when my husband and I visited my sister and brother-in-law in Guyana. It was exciting to spend time with family and friends that I haven't seen for years. Even though the atmosphere was noisy and filled with chatter and laughter, I had this strong inclination more than anything else, to visit a temple before my family and I started on our sightseeing adventures. This idea came very quickly. I never did this before and knew that this guidance came directly from the Majestic Magician who works miracles in our everyday lives which sometimes cannot be explained. A few days later, we visited the island of Trinidad and in between sightseeing, our friends took us to visit several temples. The visits didn't interfere with any of our vacation plans and I could visualize my Guru explaining to me, that this inner connection with God propelled me to visit the Holy places.

Then in my sleep one night, while still vacationing in Trinidad, I heard my Guru saying: *take pride in whatever you do. Acknowledge your achievements, whether small or grand and never underestimate the other person*. Here my Guru was advising me how to conduct myself with precision. The weather on the island was beautiful and we decided to visit one of the beaches. As I was strolling on the beach, something caught my eye. Drops of water were dripping from a small brick wall and I was perplexed as I stood there trying to figure out where the water was coming from. When I was about to walk away, I spotted a stone, the size of my palm on the wet sand next to my feet. The sand looked like someone had swept the spot where the stone was. I picked it up and while examining the stone, I was reminded of the Shiva Lingum which is a symbol of Lord Shiva that is revered by many. I returned home with the stone, thinking it was as a sacred gift from God. Surprisingly, I continued to find smaller stones in unfamiliar places, which gave me the impression, that I would see a change in my thoughts and actions.

One day, I placed all the stones that I had collected in a tray and as I stood studying the shape, size and color of each one of them, I wondered about my sudden urge and interest to collect stones. Some of them looked dull and I had this instant conviction to turn them into pieces of art. I painted the stones and was blown away by their transformation. These stones were blank canvases which displayed the vibrant colors of my life, and I could hear my Guru saying that by adding spirituality into one's life, their life can change and become filled with the colors of the Divine.

CHAPTER NINETEEN

Guru's Language

I LEARNED OVER TIME TO decipher Guru's language as I have explained that his messages came in different ways. I was drawn to a variety of things and scenarios, and after witnessing his miracles in so many ways, my way of thinking changed. Without any indication, he would surprise me and this would remind me of his presence in my life. Here are some examples that caught my attention and put a stamp in my memory.

It was summer and I had a plant pot with pansies hanging on my fence. When the plant died, I removed it from the pot. Four weeks later, I went to remove the plant pot off the fence and put it in storage for the winter season but I was surprised to find that another plant had grown with a single purple flower in bloom. The uniqueness of this plant was that it grew from a drainage hole under the pot. The plant was facing downward and when I looked again a couple of days later, the plant had managed to turn upwards.

When I saw this, I felt like the past, present and the future of my life was staring at me. My life look a unique turn with meditation and I never looked back.

Last summer, my youngest daughter was fascinated with feathers. Every time she saw a feather she took a picture. We had a few discussions about feathers, and one day, I went to the bank to make a cash deposit. I carried the cash in an envelope, and when I opened the envelope to make the deposit, there was a small white feather stuck on the inside of the envelope. Of course, I was surprised and then fascinated with the thought, that a guardian angel had accompanied me to the bank that day. At that time, my life was all about God and my Guru, which proved to me, that when you're blessed and connected to the Super Powers, their response is ongoing. In my heart, I knew that they were my Guardian Angels and I didn't feel the need to be with anyone then except my immediate family

Every morning, during the spring and summer months, I had to look at the roses and flowers in my garden, before I began walking to subway. I found it refreshing to start my day and one morning, while I was admiring the roses, these words entered my thoughts, *be a rose in the Lord's garden.* Several days later, I was looking at the roses again in my garden, when I spotted a pink rose, where half of a petal was red. The red color on the pink rose petal was so attractive, that I had to touch it to make sure that it was real. This never happened before in the past three years that I had this rose bush. I was bewildered, and when I was thinking of how this came about, a picture appeared in front of me, of all my Guru's devotees, as roses in his garden.

I woke up one morning and felt energized which was good because I wanted to complete a couple of projects around the house. In the evening, I began to prepare dinner and needed a bowl to use. I found one in the cupboard but was pleasantly startled to find a ladybug walking in the bowl. I quickly placed it among the flowers in my garden. For me, finding a lady bug in the cupboard seemed impossible and as this lingered in my thoughts, these words entered my mind, *life is good*. The following week, I went to Canada to attend a wedding and was sightseeing in the Niagara Falls area. Coincidently, when I went shopping for souvenirs, I found a plate with a lady bug and the exact words, *life is good* engraved on it. This was my Guru's playful way of always reassuring me.

On a Saturday night, I was doing my laundry and had a habit of looking for the moon. Once I saw the moon, I felt safe and protected. I always thought that the moon was watching over me when it was dark. With my laundry washed and dried, I was heading home and wanted to take a last look at the moon. When I looked up, my eyes were glued at the amazing sight in the sky. I saw white clouds in a variety of shapes and sizes in a cluster, facing the moon, and not too far away, the sky was a clear blue. I imagined the moon to be a king, and the clouds were his loyal subjects waiting to serve him. I've never had any interest in the sky or the clouds before and why now? Through constant meditation, I gained more wisdom which inspired imagination and enrichment in my life.

One night, we were driving home from an outing and almost had a terrible accident on the highway. We would have been wrong and five family members including myself would have been seriously hurt, plus the people in the other car. I was still in a state of shock and couldn't sleep. Finally, I went to bed and was about to fall asleep, when I saw the outline of a man's hand, larger than normal, reaching out to me. The hand felt incredibly soft, as it massaged my head gently. Soon after, I fell into a deep sleep and dreamt of my Guru on the highway directing traffic, while his hand was guiding us to safety. I woke up, feeling at ease, knowing that he had helped us and my worries dissipated.

Then one day when we took the children to the soccer field at pier twenty-five, I encountered a scenario where a tiny butterfly escaped death because of its quick defense mechanism. There were quite a few sparrows flying from tree to tree and chirping. This caught the attention of two of our children. They stood transfixed looking at the birds. From the flowering plants nearby, a small white butterfly appeared in front of us. One of the birds saw the butterfly and was trying to catch it. The butterfly sensed danger and tried to save its life by flying upward then downward, trying to escape. Then another bird joined in the chase and to save itself, the butterfly suddenly dived downward and went under a bench. It was fascinating to watch and seemed like I had witnessed a scene from a movie. When I think back on this incident, I realized that size and number doesn't matter, but smart thinking does.

One day, my husband and I returned home after shopping and we were really hungry. We agreed that the quickest food to prepare was sardine sandwiches. My husband emptied the sardines in a bowl and he claimed that he heard a noise. We turned over the sardines, one by one to see if there was something else in the bowl. In the oil at the bottom of the bowl we found a brand new penny. When I saw the penny, my mind began to work non-stop with questions popping up as to why and how. Still trying to figure out where the penny had come from, I went to my backyard and watered my vegetable garden. I was surprised when I saw a brand new penny next to my feet just like the one, I saw earlier in the can of sardines. I had the feeling that my Guru was advising me, to pay more importance to my eating habits, and the kind of food, I was consuming. Sooner, than I expected, I changed my diet and began eating smaller proportions and healthier foods. With good health comes happiness and so much more.

As I was returning home from the laundromat one afternoon, my eyes were drawn upwards. Instinctively, I stopped and waited. In these moments, I often wonder why my impulses, were so strong. What was so important that I had to stop and fixate my eyes on the sky line? It was as if my question was answered immediately. In the horizon, I saw ducks flying in a straight line, then changed positions and formed a narrow *V* expanding to a wider *V*. These are the simple things that I was drawn to and admired. I relished these rare finds.

One day, we were taking the children to the park, and as we were about to cross a main road, a large truck was turning toward us. A quick thinking college student instantly became our crossing guard. She stood with her back blocking the truck from moving towards us. It was an admirable gesture and we thanked her sincerely. After witnessing this incident, I thought of all the people like her, who put themselves in danger every day to help humanity.

One afternoon as I was admiring my flower garden, I noticed that one of the rose bushes had grown so much taller than the previous years. A few weeks later, I noticed that there were nine rosebuds. I was astonished because the most I'd seen were two or three in the past years. Then one day, while I was weeding the garden, I noticed that the buds were drooping a little, but the plant looked healthy. From experience, when this happens, the plant usually needs more nutrients to sustain this many roses. I began watering the plant daily, buried vegetable peelings, and added new soil around the roots. A day or two later, I saw a difference, the buds seemed healthier, and started opening up, one after the other. While I stood there, admiring the roses, a thought crept into my mind. A little TLC from above could work wonders in our lives because it is genuine and unconditional. A week later, I looked at the roses and saw that even their color had changed from a dark red, to a dark red with a tinge of purple. I felt like my Guru was showing me the positive results of paying attention, recognizing and taking steps to address deficiencies in one's life. Meditation has increased my intuitive ability to detect imbalances within myself.

For a couple of days, the temperature dropped below 33 °F and we couldn't take the children outdoors but then the temperature rose one day, and we decided to take them to a grassy area by the Hudson River. We thought that the fresh, crisp air would be a nice change for them. What we didn't know was, that the dirt was moist in some places. When it was time to return to school, we noticed that a child's brand new pink suede boots had streaks of brown mud all over the front. One of my co-workers said that we should use wipes to clean the boots. I was hesitant and was worried of making it worse. In class, I took the boots off and was going to clean them but when I looked, the mud stains were no longer there. To me it seemed as if someone had already cleaned them. I was so relieved and felt like this was a miracle. Here again, I believed that my Guru came to my rescue.

CHAPTER TWENTY

Understanding Signs

WITH MY GURU, CAME NEW opportunities to promote and expose me to everything that he thought I would benefit from. Many times I would have premonitions before things happen which was his way of alerting me to what was coming.

It was raining heavily one morning and with an umbrella over my head, I was rushing to the train station. When I was half way there, water was dripping from the umbrella and my hair was drenched. When I reached my work place, I thoroughly checked the umbrella to see if the material was damaged but it wasn't. After a couple of days, we had a leak in the first-floor bathroom and water penetrated the ceiling below. When I saw the water leaking from the ceiling, it reminded me of the water dripping on my head.

I woke up one morning and had a vision of my Guru holding a book. The next day, when I came home from work, I saw a book on my dining room table. The book was the *Bhagavad-Gita as It Is*. My husband had found it at his job and brought it home. I was anxious to read it and while I was reading this book, there were instances when I was saying to myself this was how I felt or this is what my Guru taught me. Here, I felt like I was a script writer doing research. My Guru knew that I had a lot of questions bottled in my mind and to help me solve that problem, he recommended reading spiritual literature, which would help me to understand my own voyage on the divine path. I salute all the Enlightened Beings who left these precious jewels in the form of literature for others to read and learn.

One rainy morning, on my way to work, I decided to grab our empty garbage bin from the pavement. Water from the rain formed a stream and was running down toward the sewer in front of our driveway. Something unfamiliar caught my eyes in the running water, and when I went to have a closer look, I saw dollar bills floating. I picked them up and noticed that the bills were wet and clean but the running water was really dirty. Seeing this gave me a bad feeling which prompted me to think that something was about to happen. Two days later, our car met with an accident and was badly damaged. It was costly but the insurance covered the expenses. I believed that the dirty water was an indication of the car being badly damaged and the clean money was also an indication that the insurance would cover this expense.

One Friday morning, instead of getting out of bed like I usually do, I felt lazy and stayed in bed a while longer. It was my turn to do an art activity with the kids in class that day and as I laid in bed thinking about it, I had a beautiful vision of seven colorful butterflies flying in a straight line.

Hurriedly, I got out of bed, showered, and went to work. The art activity in my classroom that morning was painting butterflies and after that I noticed, whenever I thought of a project or an activity, new ideas would rain down on me easily.

On my way to the lunch room one day, I heard a voice saying, *feel your hands*. I did and was surprised how soft and smooth they felt. When I touched the lunch room's door, it flew open. I was startled and instantly thought of my Guru's healing hands and how powerful they could be and soon after, he allowed me to demonstrate and experience the power of his hands.

One day, a friend of mine was complaining that she had a terrible headache. She said, she had taken her medication but it wasn't helping her. I offered to massage her head and forehead for a couple of minutes, and thought that maybe it would ease the pain. When I removed my hands, she commented, that she was surprised how soft my hands were. I was speechless because I know that my hands are not that soft and it brought back memories of that voice saying, *feel your hands*. An hour later, she was thanking me. Her headache was gone and she was her perky self again. I knew that this was the result of my Guru's healing energy.

I was traveling on the train one morning, and I was thinking about my new way of living, and how much I've changed, when the words, *God controls everything and makes things happen*, entered my mind. The train arrived late and all the seats were taken. I usually find it relaxing to sit in the mornings while travelling to work. This morning, I wished that someone would offer me their seat and while the thought was going through my mind, someone stood up and gave me his seat. To others, this would seem normal but to me this happened only because of my Guru's benevolent energy around me. I remember how he always looked out for me, be it something trivial or enormous and this caused my eyes to fill up with tears while my heart was consumed with gratitude.

CHAPTER TWENTY ONE

The Gift of Knowledge

ON A BEAUTIFUL SPRING DAY, we took the children to the sand park by the Hudson River. They were having fun building sand castles, going up and down the slides when my attention was drawn to a group of people standing, using their cell phones all at the same time. This scene stayed with me for a while and I thought that my Guru would be sending a message. Then my mind became a road map, busy trying to figure out what to expect. Of course, I was a bit restless and couldn't wait. On our way back to school the words, *I found light at the end of the tunnel,* crept in my mind and kept repeating themselves. To me, these words were an indication that when I retired, he would provide something for me to do. He knows me too well, I cannot sit still and not do anything.

My Guru is truly a perfect spiritual master and guide. He selflessly opened the doors of my inner world and I marveled at the wondrous beauty within. He encouraged me to meditate constantly, and this would elevate my understanding. Eventually, all my negative thoughts were slowly erased and diminished. Positivity skyrocketed in my life and my confidence was at a new high. He walked me through the tunnels of the highest knowledge, and that is to know and love God. Knowing God and loving him, is my grandest achievement. Knowing myself and my own capabilities are also an eye opening and beyond my imagination achievement. I know that this happens only once in a lifetime and the possibility of this happening again is rare. I am content and at peace with myself, which steers me away from anger, ego and selfishness. In return, I was rewarded with a greater understanding of myself and others.

One Sunday at the meditation center, I was thinking, why was I chosen to walk the path of righteousness? Was it because I wanted to serve God? My Guru appeared at the right time and took me under his shelter to show me, how to serve and receive God in my life. He helped me to understand that God is the doer.

Then early one morning, I was meditating and had a vision, which to me seemed like a graduation ceremony. I saw myself, going up in the sky and was surrounded by white clouds. A man and a woman emerged from the clouds and appeared in front of me. The man placed a crown gently on my head, and when I looked at him, it just came to me that he was God. The woman stood silently beside him, and when I tried to see who she was, I couldn't, because her face was covered. After all the uncertainty and doubts on this incredible journey, I was presented with a crown for the second time. I stood there frozen for a few seconds and then felt giddy, knowing that with the grace of my Guru, I will accomplish oneness with God.

I had this same vision in 1984 after I recovered from being really sick. I didn't know what the crown meant and on and off over the years, this vision would return to remind me of its existence, as if saying, *I am still waiting for you to grasp the meaning.* Meditation rescued me and gave me the answer. I was so relieved and marveled at the importance of meditation. My love for my Guru blossomed with gratitude and I thank him whole heartedly, for guiding me on this path. So many times, I heard him saying, *meditate, meditate and you will gain more wisdom.* I am thrilled that I listen to that voice over the years and of course, like he said, I continued to gain knowledge. This treasure, which he gives to his disciples cannot be stolen or taken away but will remain with them forever. Whenever, I think about how I was and how I am now, I want to memorize every moment, every memory, and every experience I had with him, and I wish to stay connected always with God and my Guru.

Then as the days went by, a downpour of words descended in my thoughts, describing what success means for me.

Success for me is knowing God and being connected to him,
Success for me is being healthy and obtaining peace of mind and happiness,
Success is spreading love and understanding towards society,
Success is maintaining a close relationship with my family,
Success is being able to reap the fruits of hard, honest work,
Success is being able to make the right choices.

With these words, I realized that my Guru's intervention into my life was a blessing that brought about the biggest change in me. Impossible as it seems, it's the truth. Every new day, starts with meditation, and thanking my Guru for everything he did and continues to do for me. During those times, when the divine intercepted my mind and thoughts, I remembered how I felt, what I saw and heard. My conviction then, was that God was my father and that he would take care of everything for me. I felt like I was free of all my obligations and I was happy just being in their sanctuary. My Guru and God brought integrity and a beacon of light into my life and treated me, like I was a prized piece of jewelry. I know, all of this was possible only because I was a rose in my Guru's garden in God's country.

The new me merged with the old me, and together created a peaceful and fearless individual. Divine knowledge changed me and at present, I am living my life committed to my Guru's teachings. Whenever I listened to devotional songs, I feel as if I am in a different place where only the saintly beings reside. Peace of mind, will power, happiness and good health are ingredients which helped me, to stay positive and I am using these words as my guide, respect, humility, affection for all, devotion and meditation as my anchor, understanding and common sense. My motto is do more and talk less. I am happy and I have no complaints. I never accept defeat but keep trying, always thinking that success is around the corner. I also know that I have choices and can always remove myself from any situation.

To me, words represent the rare treasures from my Guru and reshaped my life. Now, I am thinking that sometime or somewhere in my past lives, I may have sprinkled seeds in my Guru's garden, and the inner voice and the words, were the fruits he allowed me to reap. Presently, whenever I look at something new, I feel like my eyes and mind are going on an adventure and that my Guru's energy will activate my inner voice and give me acute awareness.

After gaining divine knowledge from my Guru's teachings and being exposed to spiritual knowledge through meditation, I will live my life with the following as my guiding principles.

Live my life according to my Guru's teachings,
Continue with my meditation practices and stay connected,
Learn from others,
Be reasonable and sincere,
Be gracious and understanding,
Love my children unconditionally,
Strive for peace and happiness,
Be creative and innovative,
Live the kind of life I can afford,
Enjoy life. Life is short,
Live and allow others to live,
Love God and keep him happy,
Give help without expecting anything in return.

CHAPTER TWENTY TWO

Love Conquered Me

WHEN I DISCOVERED MY INNER world, I saw love written in every nook and corner. I knew then that God and my Guru are all about love. I've never thought of its existence before and that feeling of love worked miracles with me. It gave me the enthusiasm to venture out to do and see things which never interest me before. I thrived knowing that God resides in my inner world, and this gave me the tenacity that I could achieve anything, I set my mind on. I felt, like I could climb the highest mountain without any fear. I became aware that within me is a pure soul and imagined myself as a blank piece of paper with the word *love* penned across it. I know that I am loved by God and my Guru.

On a mild summer day, I was returning from the laundromat and was humming a devotional song on my way home. My heart was consumed with love for God and my Guru, when I heard that soft toned voice from within asking a question. *What is love?* This question was sudden and unexpected as usual. After thinking about this question for days, I've decided that I would write something unique to describe the kind of love, I was exposed to, as my Guru's disciple. Then one day, while I was having my breakfast and still thinking about this question, I became overwhelmed with love for my father. My father died years ago and to me this was strange, because I've never felt like this before. I knew that when anything out of the ordinary occurs, it meant something. A week later, I met a relative of mine and was telling her how I felt and during our conversation, I encountered the same feeling, only this time, I was thinking about my Guru. I couldn't believe how intense this feeling was. I think my Guru was making me aware of the kind of love, a Guru showers on his disciples. After this incredible experience, I had a gut feeling that this phase in my life would end soon. My Guru's story started with love and is ending with an explanation of the strong bond that exists between a Guru and his disciples. A few days later, words arrived cascading from above, like a water fall into my thoughts and they were:

Love from my Guru is pure, innocent, and incomparable. His love is like a river that over flows beyond its boundaries to give me courage, peace of mind, and independence. This feeling engulfed my whole being and changed my way of thinking. His pure, unconditional love is like a magnet which pulls at the heartstrings of his disciples. Adoration for my Guru grew, as he travelled with me on this journey of self-realization. I looked at simple, everyday things and fell in love with them. The ducks flying and forming letters on the skyline. A rose on the very first day the petals opened.

Birds looking for worms in a grassy field. Pigeons resting in City Hall Park, and to my astonishment, a crane on my front lawn in Florida calling out to me. I felt love and admiration by just looking, seeing and hearing. I never knew this kind of love exists, but with my Guru, I was exposed to greater depths of thinking and feelings which changed my perception in life.

My Guru was compassionate and under his care, I was free from negative thoughts, ignorance and worries. It felt so good. He was on my mind, in my thoughts and in my heart all the time. There was no space for ego and ignorance, as he continued relentlessly with me on this path to higher knowledge. Just imagine, standing beside God, observing yourself with others and heard him asking questions and giving answers. How would you feel, when God placed his hand on your head, after a hard days' work and gave you his blessings because he was pleased? How would you feel knowing who he was, when you walked with him and held his pinky finger? That was how I felt, like royalty, just being with him. Sometimes I cried and other times, I was inspired to write letters of gratitude and prayers as I continued to praise and thank him in silence.

CHAPTER TWENTY THREE

Inspirational Letters And Prayers

FILLED WITH IMMENSE GRATITUDE, I wanted to do something for my Guru because of all the incredible things he did for me. With a strong feeling of sincere adoration, came the determination to write these letters and prayers for him. When I witnessed all the miracles, saw the visions, heard the voice from within, received the words falling from above, his teachings and guidance on this path, I knew that I had all these experiences only because my Guru is a perfect spiritual master. A true enlightened Guru who imparts his divine knowledge and allows his disciples to know God and their true self. I've never had any inspiration in the past to write prayers or letters of this kind but now, I have so many. Words flowed effortlessly, and fulfilled my wishes.

Dear Guru,

Please give me the words to write and share my experiences with the world. I want to describe in detail the precious moments I spent with you. I can't forget the images, I saw of myself as a little girl, holding on to your pinky finger and walking with you. I wish for others to experience what it was like to be in the company with someone of your caliber. My hope is that this story will inspire them to discover divinity from within, and once they've found it, hold on to it and never let go.

With sincere wishes.

This is my thank you letter to my Guru, who showered his blessings on me, to show me a new way, to live my life.

Dear Guru,

I want to thank you for giving me the insight to think, act and see things differently. I also want to thank you for recognizing that rare and unique quality that I didn't know existed within me. As your student, you brought light into my life. You taught me how to survive during difficult times and to think and act with dignity. Having you as my teacher was a mind boggling experience, one that I will never forget. You encouraged me to work diligently and my achievements soared to greater heights. You were my inspiration. You came into my life, taught and trained me with enthusiasm, patience and calmness. Your methods of teachings were much more advanced than the ones I was accustomed to. I was never afraid, stressed or tired but was eagerly waiting in suspense for the next lesson. Because of your tolerance and guidance, I was able to digest your teachings and conquered my fears and vices. My confidence grew steadfastly and reached new heights. You gave me higher knowledge and injected the traits of independence because you knew this would work best for me. I know that you are not an ordinary person. You are bigger and greater than life. A saintly king who is helping humanity. A genuine and precious gift to mankind. You are cherished by so many.

Your voice has an attraction that no one can resist. It's a voice that turn heads and compels an audience. I worship you. Your burst of energy, allows me to become fearless, patient, self-sufficient and creative. You are my sun, my moon, my everlasting brightly lit lamp and my pillar of strength. You are my star, my sparkling diamonds and my antique radio that plays devotional songs. Listening to the songs always make me feel close to God and you, my Guru.

I cannot thank you enough and I will never forget you. You have a special place in my heart and my promise to you my Guru, is that I will walk the path of righteous, for the rest of my life. I saw my true potential when you took the form of Lord Rama. Your memory will always be with me.

With sincere thanks and affection,
Your devotee.

Dear Guru,

I thank you for teaching me that truth is the best path to thread on.
I thank you for taking your precious time to train and show me that I have choices.
I thank you for having faith in me.
I thank you for inspiring me to follow in your footsteps.
I thank you for being strict with me. I learned.
I thank you for guiding me on this journey and because of you, I completed it with flying colors.
I thank you for being my key, you opened the door and allowed me to enter my inner world.
I thank you sincerely and will always be grateful.

Dear Guru,

There are so many who sacrificed their lives for you and yet you chose me. Why my Guru? In the end you gave me more than I deserved. Father, you want us to do well and you want us to live decent and progressive lives. You want us to be happy, healthy and independent individuals. You want us to be respectful and affectionate with one another. The good news is, I see people changing for the better every day because they want to. They need encouragement, guidance and confidence. You're the only one who can make this happen. Please help us all.

Dear Guru,

Thank you, thank you, and thank you,
Thank you for selecting me to be in your shelter,
Thank you for giving me opportunities to become bigger than life,
Thank you for giving me permission to write about my experiences with you,
Thank you for your blessings and the freedom to do what is right, under the scrutiny of your watchful eyes,
Thank you for the once-in-a-lifetime experiences,

Thank you for taking the time to teach and educate me,

Thank you for changing me from a meek mouse into a roaring lion,

Thank you for always believing in me,

Thank you for showing me the difference between right and wrong,

Thank you for giving me hope and teaching me how to be independent,

Thank you for creating and exposing me to situations where I was able to solve them peacefully,

Thank you for listening,

Thank you for giving me the sun, the moon, and the wind as my companions and security guard,

Thank you for the visions of Lord Krishna and Lord Shiva. I was sleeping, and when I woke up, I saw them hovering over me,

Thank you for all the people you chose as actors to help me on this journey,

Thank you for being so considerate, I don't have to worry anymore,

Thank you for protecting me, my family, my relatives, and my friends,

Thank you for lighting up the streets as I walked,

Thank you for giving me some of what you have so that I can see, hear, and feel like you do,

Thank you for trusting me and showing me
light at the end of the tunnel,
What have I done, Father, to deserve such
an incredible honor? You made me see the
world through your eyes and taught me
how to rise.

Dear Guru,

Give me the wisdom to face the world,
Give me the wisdom to think before I act,
Give me the wisdom to choose my friends
wisely,
Give me the wisdom to feel empathy for
others,
Give me the wisdom to remain calm at all
times,
Give me the wisdom to help others,
Give me the wisdom to change the negatives
into positives,
Give me the wisdom to be honest,
Give me the wisdom to create friends
instead of enemies,
Give me the wisdom to move forward.

After I retired, I knew that it was the right time to
focus and start writing this story. Surprisingly, as I was
writing, the meanings of his messages and teachings began
to unfold, which gave me a better understanding of my
Guru's mission. All the answers to my many questions were
revealed, as I meditated constantly while I was studying and
thinking how to present this story. When I wrote the story,

I realized that meditation is the secret wand which connects a disciple to the Guru and through this connection, the Guru reveals the truth of one's existence and the divine. My Guru, the perfect, enlightened, spiritual master, conveys all kinds of knowledge to his disciples on this path. So many times, when the spiritual understanding was revealed, I was speechless. I didn't do anything, to deserve him in my life and I can still see myself sitting alone in a classroom, with my Guru standing next to a chalk board teaching me.